A YEAR OF Gingerbread Houses

Kristine Samuell

MAKING & DECORATING
GINGERBREAD HOUSES FOR ALL SEASONS

D1225941

New York

An Imprint of Sterling Publishing
1166 Avenue of the Americas
New York, NY 10036

LARK CRAFTS and the distinctive Lark logo are registered trademarks of Sterling Publishing Co., Inc.

Text and illustrations © 2015 by Kristine Samuell
Photography © 2015 by Lark Crafts

All rights reserved. No part of this publication may be reproduced, stored in a retrieval system,
or transmitted in any form or by any means (including electronic, mechanical, photocopying, recording,
or otherwise) without prior written permission from the publisher.

ISBN 978-1-4547-0891-9

Distributed in Canada by Sterling Publishing
c/o Canadian Manda Group, 664 Annette Street
Toronto, Ontario, Canada M6S 2C8
Distributed in the United Kingdom by GMC Distribution Services
Castle Place, 166 High Street, Lewes, East Sussex, England BN7 1XU
Distributed in Australia by Capricorn Link (Australia) Pty. Ltd.
P.O. Box 704, Windsor, NSW 2756, Australia

For information about custom editions, special sales, and premium and corporate purchases,
please contact Sterling Special Sales at 800–805–5489 or specialsales@sterlingpublishing.com.

Manufactured in China

2 4 6 8 10 9 7 5 3 1

larkcrafts.com

www.TheGingerbreadJournal.com

*To
Mom*

Your creative, charming, and
flawless creations graced our home,
and our hearts, every year.

Contents

Introduction

Gingerbread smells like home to me. Christmas at our house revolved around my mother's dazzling gingerbread creations. As a young child I likened the gingerbread season to the story of the Elves and the Shoemaker. We would wake up each morning to a spicy warm smell, and rush out to see what Mom had made during the night. When we were old enough to help, Mom wrapped us in aprons and discovered that the three of us could create half the number of houses in twice the time. The mess was incalculable. My sister and I, delighted to participate, did our best to contain the cloud of powdered sugar billowing from the mixing bowl. Mom's houses were marvels of perfection—each line of icing straight, each candy exactly positioned, all colors coordinated, with several new designs each year. We created gingerbread structures solely for strength. The stronger the house, the more candy it could support. And what is more wonderful than a simple gingerbread house encased and encrusted with every color and form of candy?

Forty years later, I discovered the intricate piping work that pastry artists in the Czech Republic and other parts of Eastern Europe use to decorate gingerbread year-round. Inspired by the simple beauty of delicate white icing swirled over dark, glossy cookies I set out to learn the art of piping. I scoured websites for recipes, ideas, patterns, and instructions. Photographs from around the world inspired me to practice piping. I started with dot patterns and progressed, very slowly, to scrolls and flourishes. My philosophy evolved—make a mistake, cover it with a gumdrop. Make a bigger mistake, add a tree or a gingerbread man. What a wonderful, fragrant canvas I had on which to practice—friends, relatives, neighbors, and teachers gobbled up my successes and failures alike.

A gingerbread house engages all of the senses. As you read, decide which aspects of the gingerbread experience you enjoy most. If architectural design is appealing, invent your own splendid structure. Color enthusiasts can compose candy into vibrant arrays or luminous pastel palettes. If the smell of cinnamon and ginger stirs your soul, add extra spices to the dough and don't miss the recipe for gingersnaps on page 10. Whether you complete one of the following projects or design and create your own, you and your family can enjoy a gingerbread masterpiece.

Part One

Learning
·the·
Basics

Your Masterpiece

You'll need only some cookies and a little icing to create a basic gingerbread house. This white-on-brown simplicity can be charming. Add candy, an icing flourish, or landscaping and you're off on a gingerbread adventure. Before we talk about beauty, let's talk about the structure itself. Four things are necessary for a wonderful gingerbread house experience:

◆ A rigid, food-safe base to support the house

◆ Solid, strong gingerbread pieces that will support themselves and the goodies you attach

◆ Royal icing at the proper consistencies (thick for assembly, thinner for decorations)

◆ Adequate time, including time for drying

PLANNING A GINGERBREAD HOUSE

Making a gingerbread house almost always requires more than one day because the icing must dry after each step. You may be tempted to hurry things along, but always keep in mind the four requirements. Setting

Fig. 1

your gingerbread house under or in front of a fan speeds drying. If you need a quick project, check out our hints for time-savers.

This is the general flow of a gingerbread project:

- Choose a pattern. Make pattern pieces from paper or thin cardboard.
- Find a sturdy base.
- Assemble tools and ingredients.
- Prepare the gingerbread construction dough.
- Roll the dough and cut out the house pieces.
- Bake and cool the cookies.
- Make the royal icing.
- Decorate the front, back, and side walls and let them dry thoroughly.
- Assemble the four walls (not the roof) and let them dry.
- Attach the roof and allow it to dry.
- Decorate the roof, base, and landscaping and allow it to dry.

TIME-SAVERS FOR THE BUSY DECORATOR

There are many shortcuts available if you're pressed for time.

To shorten the time required for projects in this book, consider building a smaller house. If the house pictured is enlarged 200 percent, you could enlarge the pattern 150 percent or not at all.

Replace items modeled from fondant with purchased candies.

Make your house look bigger by putting it on a smaller base. Use an overturned plate or platter for more height. This also adds a bit of elegant curve to the grass or snow.

Surround the house with a multitude of candies instead of creating trees and décor with icing or pastillage. It's hard to go wrong with candy!

The standard gingerbread house kits available in stores make excellent starting points if you prefer not to bake. Discard the premade icing. Decorate and assemble the house with your own royal icing and extra candies. Some houses come already assembled. I find it difficult to pipe on vertical walls, but this could make an excellent house for children to decorate. Factory-made houses tend to be quite sturdy and can withstand mountains of candy.

You can cut graham crackers to make small (and somewhat fragile) houses. If you want to create one

Fig. 2

of these, cut two of each of the house pieces. Use royal icing to sandwich two fronts together, two backs together, and so on. This doubles the strength of your graham crackers (Fig. 1).

You can build a large house from graham crackers using a cardboard box cut into the shape of a house. The box provides all of the structural support. Use royal icing as glue and completely cover it in graham crackers. Some crackers will need to be trimmed to the proper shape. After the royal icing has completely dried, add the decorations and candy. These graham crackers should not be eaten because they've been up against the box, but all of the candy is fair game.

Create a two-dimensional house by making only the house front. Decorate the front as you wish, let it dry, and prop it up for display. Plate stands can support some cookies. Larger cookies will need to lean against something solid or be supported by back braces. These are elongated triangles and stand at right angles to the cookie. You can make these from gingerbread or corrugated cardboard (Fig. 2).

USING NON-EDIBLES ON A GINGERBREAD HOUSE

Gingerbread house competitions require all parts of the house and decorations to be edible. This makes good sense for any gingerbread house. It looks and smells delicious, and it's encrusted with candy so people may eat it, with or without your knowledge!

Take special care if you have children or pets. They will—trust me—eat, or try to eat, from the house. Dogs in particular find gingerbread irresistible. Curly ribbon, toy animals or cars, and cellophane wrapping can all be dangerous to small children and animals.

There are several confectionery items the FDA has not approved that you may choose to put on your house. Silver dragées and disco dust add sparkle and shine but have not been FDA approved for consumption. Candy canes melt if exposed to air, so the candy canes on my houses are still tightly wrapped in cellophane or made from fondant. Warn your family about anything on the house that can't be eaten, and be very specific about this if you give a house away.

DESIGNING THE HOUSE

Gingerbread houses are a brilliant creative outlet for adults, a fun afternoon for kids, or a special holiday tradition for families. Design a house that satisfies your goals.

Consider:
✦ Size
✦ Complexity—simple architecture or elaborate touches such as

dormers, bay windows, etc.
✦ Decorations—minimalist candy, fancy icing designs, loads of candy, a particular theme, colors
✦ Time—how much time you want to devote to the house

Choose to spend time on those aspects you most enjoy. An avid baker or architect might revel in complex plans and construction. I most enjoy the decorating, so my houses are cut from simple patterns. When choosing a size, remember that the decorations and landscaping will add height and heft to your house.

CHOOSING A PATTERN

The choice of patterns from books, magazines, and blogs is endless, and should you not find what you want, simply design your own. The Resources section lists several books and websites for further inspiration.

All of the houses in this book are made from patterns in the appendix.

These patterns can be photocopied and enlarged as you wish. Each project specifies the percentage that I enlarged the pattern to create the pictured house. This is only a guideline—enlarge less and create a smaller project; enlarge more and create a gargantuan house.

Remember that the house itself is only the beginning; the height of the base, roof décor, and candies will add size and weight to the finished project (Fig. 3).

CUTTING PATTERN PIECES

Cut pattern pieces from paper or thin cardboard such as poster board or cereal box cardboard. If your pattern needs to be enlarged, do so with a copy machine, then cut out the pattern pieces. If you're using the pattern only once, stick with the paper pattern. Otherwise, trace the paper pieces onto thin cardboard and cut them out. Label each pattern piece to help identify baked gingerbread pieces.

Fig. 3

Equipment

You don't need a lot of fancy equipment to bake and decorate a gingerbread house. You likely have most or all of the tools in your kitchen already.

BASIC REQUIRED EQUIPMENT

Gingerbread dough can be mixed with a **stand mixer** or by hand. Stand mixers quickly and easily whip up wonderful bowls of royal icing. If you must use a hand mixer for icing, make only a half recipe and use a large bowl. Keeping the beaters immersed only in shallow icing eases the strain on the motor. In a pinch, you can mix small amounts of royal icing in a coffee cup.

A **rolling pin** is needed for rolling dough.

A large, flat **surface** on a table or countertop is best for your work area.

A **pizza cutter** is used to cut dough—the smaller the wheel, the better, because you can cut more precisely. Alternately, use a small sharp knife.

A **turner** (pancake spatula) with a tapered, sharp edge is needed to slide under the dough. Some turners have blunt, boxlike edges that push and distort the dough instead of slipping underneath it.

Pattern pieces cut from paper or cereal-box cardboard guide you in cutting the shapes you need.

I prefer insulated aluminum **baking sheets**, but any flat baking sheets will do. Keep in mind that dark or thin baking sheets can burn the bottoms of your cookies. If this happens, reduce the temperature of the oven.

An **icing spatula** with a flexible head scrapes clean the sides of the mixing bowl.

Piping bags are available in several forms:

+ Disposable plastic piping bags are quick and inexpensive. Use a bag once, remove the decorating tip, and throw it away.
+ Parchment cornets are another disposable option.
+ Reusable featherweight plastic piping bags are worth the investment if you plan to make more than a few gingerbread houses. Any reusable piping bags you plan to use with royal icing should be labeled ROYAL ICING ONLY, because even minute amounts of fat will destroy royal icing. Mark royal icing bags at the top edge with permanent marker.

Rubber bands or bag ties are used to secure icing in the bag.

Parchment cones can be folded out of parchment paper (see Making Parchment Cornets, page 27).

A **dinner plate** makes a fantastic resting place for the spatula. It contains the icing and speeds cleanup; just soak the plate and the icing dissolves.

A strong, rigid **base** will support your gingerbread house and all of its décor.

RECOMMENDED EQUIPMENT

Roll large pieces of gingerbread directly onto **parchment paper**. Remove the extra dough, cut the paper around the cookies, and transfer them straight to a baking sheet. Cut parchment paper into large triangles for folding paper cornets.

Meringue powder is powdered egg white mixed with some powdered sugar and cornstarch. Meringue powder makes a wonderfully fluffy and quick-crusting royal icing.

Decorating tips are metal or plastic cones with various openings.

A **coupler** is a plastic piece that goes inside a decorating bag to make a universal attachment for different tips. A second ring screws on the outside of the tip to keep it attached. Couplers allow you to change tips without emptying the icing out of the bag.

Several brands of **gel or paste food coloring** are available. Liquid food coloring (commonly found in a four pack at the grocery store) adds too much water to your icing and should not be used.

Candies come in thousands of varieties. Your imagination is the limit!

Placing your house beneath an overhead **fan**, or in the path of a portable fan, will dry the icing much more quickly.

Toothpicks are used to remove an icing mistake, add paste food coloring, spread flood icing, and so much more.

MY FAVORITE TOOLS
Please see the Resources section (page 131) for specific manufacturers and suppliers.

A **plastic dough scraper** is used to scrape bowls, knead dough, clean the counter, coax icing down toward the tip of the bag—the list goes on and on.

Use a **craft knife** to cut intricate details in gingerbread or fondant.

Impression mats give texture to dough, fondant, and pastillage. My favorite type is made by FMM and gives gingerbread dough and pastillage a wood grain or cobblestone effect.

Cutters make easy work of cutting shapes. I use several kinds:

- Special shapes, such as the scalloped fence on page 61, use the FMM Straight Frill Cutter Set 9–12.
- Flowers such as the daisies on page 94 are made with daisy plunger cutters from various manufacturers.
- Kemper cutters are used for small shapes such as the windows on Louisa's Bakery. They come in different shapes, such as circles, hearts, and flowers.
- Nested sets of graduated round, square, and oval cutters are handy for cutting these basic shapes.

A small **offset spatula**, with or without a tapered end, will help spread icing.

Use a **plastic ruler** as a straight edge or for centering decorations.

Silicone molds are used for special embellishments such as the white fondant birds on page 71.

Waxed paper is used as a base on which to form and dry royal icing creations

Always have an extra bag of **powdered sugar** on hand, because success depends on creating icing of the correct consistency.

A **nontoxic graphite pencil or large corsage pin** is used for marking on gingerbread.

Nonslip shelf liner keeps gingerbread pieces and bases from moving on the table.

A **double-ended pottery tool**, my favorite tool, is used for many things. The metal endpieces are tiny, sharp, and maneuvrable.

Shot glasses or cappuccino cups are handy for mixing small amounts of icing.

PME piping tips No. 00, No. 0, and No. 1 are available at specialty cake decorating shops or online (see Resources, page 131). These stainless steel tips are seamless, so they pipe a straighter line of icing.

The Base

A gingerbread house needs a strong, stable base that can support the weight of the house, icing, and candy. If the base bends, the royal icing on top of it can fracture or the entire house could break away.

Many things could be used as a base. Although you may have them in your cupboard, consider using an older item or buying a spare from the thrift store:

- A white or glass plate turned upside down
- A cutting board
- A glass plate from an unused microwave
- Stacked, foil-covered cardboard circles
- Purchased cake drums
- Upside down pie pans, 9 × 13 pans, etc.
- A lazy susan
- Plywood

MAKING A CARDBOARD OR PLYWOOD BASE

Because you can buy a second-hand or discount store plate inexpensively, I consider cardboard bases a last resort. Some houses with interior lighting require an access hole in the middle of the base and should be constructed with plywood or cardboard. Bigger houses require bases larger than a platter, and plywood is ideal for this situation. Read the Lighting section (page 96) to determine if and how you might light your house.

Any surface that is porous or not food-safe needs to be covered. Heavy-duty foil is shiny, reasonably tough, and inexpensive. Clear packing tape holds the extra foil securely to the underside of the base.

The foil must act as a second skin to your base. It should be securely and tightly wrapped so it can't tear loose. Any play or wrinkles in the foil can allow your house to move, and the house's own weight can rip the foil right off the base.

Cardboard Base

Here is how to most effectively construct a cardboard base covered with foil.

Materials

+ Cardboard cake circles or stiff, clean corrugated cardboard,

Fig. 4

something round to trace the circles, marker pen, and sharp knife

+ Hot glue gun with glue sticks
+ Heavy-duty aluminum foil
+ Clear packing tape

Trace circles onto the cardboard using a plate, large bowl, or compass as a guide. The bigger the base, the more layers of cardboard you will need to support the weight of a bigger house. When you have the circles cut out, look at the lines formed by the corrugation. Hot glue the circles on top of each other with the lines at varying angles (this will make a stronger base than if the lines are all parallel). When cool, tightly wrap the base in heavy foil. Turn the base over so the wrong side is up and trim any extra foil that might make the base lumpy or uneven. Use clear packing tape to secure the foil to the back of the base (Fig. 4). On larger bases, I also encircle the entire base with an additional belt of tape to strengthen the foil.

Plywood Base

Plywood cut into squares or circles is covered in the same way as cardboard. After wrapping the board and taping the excess foil to the underside of it, use clear packing tape to strengthen the foil. Make one complete wrap around the board as you would with ribbon around a package. Turn the board ninety degrees, then make another wrap, as if drawing a plus sign on the base.

Basic Recipes

Gingerbread houses require a strong, dense, and sturdy cookie that will support the weight of icing and candies. This recipe for construction-grade gingerbread is strong and tough and smells wonderful. A tastier recipe follows for gingerbread cookies that are to be decorated and eaten.

GINGERBREAD FOR CONSTRUCTION

This recipe holds its shape well during baking and resists rising or spreading. Traditionally, gingerbread contains molasses, but my recipe substitutes corn syrup and honey for part of the molasses. The honey hardens the cookie, and the corn syrup lightens its color. Use different proportions of corn syrup and molasses to change the dough's color. One full cup of light corn syrup will yield lighter dough; one full cup of molasses makes the dough quite dark. Gingerbread cookies have a longer shelf life than other rolled cookies, because they contain a relatively small proportion of fat.

½ cup butter (4 ounces)
1 cup sugar (7 ounces)
⅓ cup light corn syrup (4 ounces)
⅓ cup molasses (4 ounces)
⅓ cup honey (4 ounces)
4 teaspoons ginger
2 tablespoons cinnamon
1 teaspoon salt
½+ cup water
6+ cups all purpose flour
  (27 ounces)

Cream the butter and sugar. Beat in the corn syrup, molasses, honey, ginger, cinnamon, and salt. Add the flour and water slowly, alternating between them. Knead the dough, adding more flour or water as needed. The dough should be stiff enough for rolling. If you prefer, chill the dough before rolling. Bake at 300–350°F on parchment or a lightly greased baking sheet. Baking time is highly dependent upon the thickness of the cookie.

Dough Color Variations

LIGHTER DOUGH

✦ Substitute 1 cup light corn syrup for the corn syrup, honey, and molasses.

✦ Add 2 teaspoons vanilla.

✦ Increase the ginger to 6 teaspoons and reduce the cinnamon to 1 tablespoon.

DARKER DOUGH
(full flavor, spicy gingerbread)

✦ Substitute 1 cup molasses for the corn syrup, honey, and molasses.

✦ Increase ginger and cinnamon as taste allows. I use 4 tablespoons cinnamon and 6 heaping teaspoons of ginger. Add 1 teaspoon ground cloves.

COLORED DOUGH

✦ For the black dough used for the Haunted Hideaway, make a recipe of the darker dough gingerbread and add black food coloring.

✦ For dough of other colors, make a recipe of the lighter dough gingerbread and add food coloring. The light brown color of the dough will influence your resulting color.

GINGERSNAPS FOR EATING

You can bake this dough into soft cookies or the harder snaps. Adjust the amount of ginger to suit your palate. The four teaspoons of ginger create a cookie with universal appeal but double this amount for true spice lovers.

¾ cup shortening (4.9 ounces)
1 cup brown sugar, packed
  (8 ounces)
1 egg
¼ cup molasses (3 ounces)
1 teaspoon cloves
1 tablespoon cinnamon
4 teaspoons ginger
2¼ cup flour (10.1 ounces)
¼ teaspoon salt
2 teaspoons baking soda

Cream the shortening and sugar. Mix in the egg, molasses, cloves, cinnamon, and ginger. Combine the flour, salt, and baking soda and blend in. Chill the dough for 1 hour. Roll the dough into walnut-sized balls, then roll the balls in sugar. Bake on parchment or a greased cookie sheet at 375°F for 8–10 minutes. Remove while still soft. The tops will crinkle. For crisp gingersnaps, bake for 10–15 minutes.

GINGERBREAD BOYS AND GIRLS FOR EATING

Use the recipe for soft gingersnaps with these changes: Increase the flour to 3 cups (13.5 ounces), the salt to 1 teaspoon, and leave out the baking soda. Add 3 tablespoons of water to the creamed ingredients before adding the dry ingredients. Bake at 325–350°F on parchment or a greased cookie sheet. Baking times will vary with cookie thickness.

SPRITZ BUTTER COOKIES

Spritz cookie dough is traditionally squeezed with a cookie press into stars, flowers, trees, and other shapes. This recipe has less flour than most, and the room temperature dough should be pliable enough to pipe through a large decorating tip.

1½ cups butter, room temperature
  (12 ounces)
1 cup sugar (7 ounces)
1 egg, room temperature
1 teaspoon vanilla
1 teaspoon almond extract
  (real, not imitation)
3½ cups flour (15.7 ounces)
1 teaspoon baking powder

Cream the butter and sugar together. Add the egg and beat until fluffy. Add the vanilla and almond extract. Mix in 1 cup of flour and the baking powder. Slowly add the remaining 2½ cups of flour. Pipe the room temperature dough through a disposable piping bag with a large tip or chill the dough and use a cookie press. Bake at 375°F for 6–10 minutes.

Spritz cookie dough is traditionally squeezed with a cookie press into stars, flowers, trees, and other shapes. This recipe has less flour than most, and the room temperature dough should be pliable enough to pipe through a large decorating tip.

EDIBLE GLUE

TIP: Tylose powder is available at cake decorating stores and online.

1 tablespoon warm water
1 pinch (around ⅛ teaspoon)
  tylose powder

Put the warm water in a small sealable container, shot glass, or egg cup. Add the tylose powder. Use a paintbrush or toothpick to stir until all of the tylose breaks up and is absorbed. Let the mixture sit for a few hours until it reaches the consistency of honey. It may look slightly pink but should dry clear.

PASTILLAGE

Pastillage dries rock hard and is often used for construction or support elements. The finished texture is much like conversation hearts or tinned strong mint candies. Because it dries completely, you can create items in advance and store them. People around the world mean different things when they say fondant, pastillage, or sugar paste. In this book, just remember that fondant (which I purchase premade) stays somewhat soft,

while this homemade pastillage
dries rock hard.

¼ cup hot water (2 ounces)
¾ tablespoon of unflavored
    powdered gelatin (1 packet)
½ cup cornstarch (2 ounces)
4 cups powdered sugar (1 pound)
¼ teaspoon cream or tartar

Put the hot water into a small bowl.
Sprinkle the powdered gelatin over
the top of the water. Allow it to sit
for a few minutes, then use a spatula
to thoroughly blend the mixture and
smash out any lumps. Combine the
cornstarch, 3 cups of the powdered
sugar, and the cream of tartar in
a mixing bowl. Make a well in
the center and pour in the watery
gelatin. Mix with a stand mixer or
by hand with a large spoon. Knead
the dough until smooth and elastic,
using powdered sugar to stiffen it
and water to loosen it as needed.
Form the pastillage into a ball and
cover it with a thin layer of white
shortening. Store pastillage very
tightly wrapped in plastic or sealed
in an airtight container with plastic
wrap over the surface of the dough.
It will become smoother if allowed
to rest overnight.

Baking
the
House

You have the pattern pieces cut
out, dough mixed, and baking
equipment ready. It's time to bake.

ROLLING & CUTTING

I use two methods to roll, cut, and
bake gingerbread houses, depending
on the size of the piece.

Fig. 5

I roll large pieces directly on
a piece of parchment paper. I use
the pattern piece to cut the cookie,
remove the extra dough, then cut the
parchment paper before transferring
each piece (on it's parchment) to
baking sheets.

I roll small pieces on a lightly
floured counter and use a pancake
spatula to transfer these pieces to
the baking sheet. Many small pieces
easily transfer without distortion,
but sometimes you'll need to
re-trim on the baking sheet using
the pattern.

Divide a recipe of dough and
form each half into a flat square.
This helps keep the rolled dough

Fig. 6

Fig. 7

in more of a rectangular shape. You can cut more pieces from a rectangular piece of dough than from a circular piece (Fig. 5).

Roll the dough ¼–½ inch thick. Larger houses with larger pieces will need the thicker dough. Your house *must* be structurally sound with hard walls! The cookies forming the front, back, and sides (vertical pieces) will support the weight of the roof, decorations, and candy. Decorative pieces such as shutters, shingles, doors, etc. can be rolled as thinly or as thickly as you please.

Rolling and Cutting the Dough on Parchment Paper

Roll and cut large pieces on parchment paper. Before laying the parchment down, wipe the counter with a clean damp rag. The thin film of water will keep the parchment paper from slipping. Lightly flour the parchment and your rolling pin so the dough can move and expand in all directions. Roll the dough to a ¼–½ inch thickness. If the dough has extra flour on top, brush it aside. If the dough is shiny and slick, you may need to spread a small amount of flour on top to keep the pattern piece from sticking.

Lay the pattern pieces on the dough and trim around them with a pizza cutter or sharp knife. Remove the extra dough, then snip the paper between gingerbread pieces and slide each onto the baking sheet (Fig. 6). The cookies keep their shapes perfectly during the transfer. Silicone mats work with this method, too, but you can't cut the mat into pieces to fit more on a baking sheet.

Rolling and Cutting the Dough without Parchment Paper

Sprinkle a little flour over your rolling surface. Sprinkle additional flour in the very middle of the space.

As you roll the dough, you push it outward from the center and flour is incorporated into it at the same time. Extra flour in the middle of your work area can keep the center of the dough from sticking while reducing the total amount of flour added to the dough.

Roll the dough ¼–½ inch thick. Lay a cardboard pattern piece on top, leaving a ½ inch margin around all sides. Cut outside the ½ inch margin with a pizza cutter to make a piece of dough bigger than your pattern piece.

Small cookies can go directly onto a cool, greased baking sheet with a pancake spatula. Move bigger cookies using one of the large cardboard pattern pieces. Slide the cardboard under the dough to fully support it and lift the gingerbread to the baking sheet. The baking sheet now holds roughly cut cookies. Trim each cookie again using a pizza cutter or small knife to trim precisely around the edge of the pattern (Fig. 7). Remove the extra dough and you should have a gingerbread cookie exactly the shape and size of your pattern piece.

If your design calls for open windows or doors, cut them now using small cutters or a sharp knife.

BAKING

Bake gingerbread house pieces until they are tough and hard. Start with the oven at 350°F, but reduce the temperature to 325°F or even 300°F for thicker or very large cookies. Gingerbread dough browns as it bakes. Reduce the temperature to keep the cookies from darkening too much. Baking times range from 7 to 30 minutes, depending on the oven, humidity, and thickness of the dough.

A gingerbread cookie ready to come out of the oven will have slightly browned edges and a firm center. Cool the pieces and check them again. The cookies must be completely hard. Soft spots often hide in the center of the cookie's back. When all of my pieces are cooled, I check each one and set aside any with soft areas. If the cookies are soft, bake them again.

I use several methods to re-bake or harden gingerbread house pieces. One method is to return them to the oven at a lower temperature of 275–300°F. Watch carefully to prevent excess browning.

A second method is to load the baking sheets solid with cookies (the pieces will no longer bake into each other) and put them in an oven heated to 200°F for an extended time. This low heat dehydrates the cookies and shouldn't darken them.

The final method is to load the cookie sheets with gingerbread pieces and leave them in the oven as it cools, once you are completely done baking. If you do this, tape a note to the oven controls to make certain that the oven isn't turned on again with the cookies still inside!

GLAZING

An egg glaze adds shine and color to your finished gingerbread. Use egg glaze on doors, shutters, fireplaces or other small items to make them stand out, or glaze all of the pieces to create a gleaming, shiny gingerbread house. Remove the white and chalaza bits from an egg and beat only the yolk with 1 tablespoon of heavy cream or milk. Brush this on a fully baked gingerbread cookie. Return it to the oven for 3–5 minutes to dry the glaze.

MAKING CURVED GINGERBREAD

If your project requires curved pieces, you have two options. Slight curves for a rounded roof can be made after the cookie is baked. Gently bend the warm, pliable cookie into the shape you want and hold it until cool. More dramatic

Fig. 8

curves require some type of mold during baking. Lightly grease the mold. To form a bridge, crumple up aluminum foil that will shape the void under the bridge. Cover this with a smooth piece of foil so the cookie is easily removed after baking. Lay the gingerbread dough across the hump, bake, cool, and remove the foil (Fig. 8).

EMBOSSING GINGERBREAD

Impression mats mold gingerbread pieces with many textured patterns. I love using wood grain textures for doors and shutters and cobblestone textures for walkways, bridges, and fireplaces. It's a simple way to add whimsy or sophistication to your house.

Roll the gingerbread dough ⅓ inch thick and coat the top with a light dusting of flour. Dip the textured surface of the mold into flour and tap it to remove the extra. Place the mold on the dough and roll the rolling pin over it once using moderate pressure (Fig. 9). Carefully peel the mold away and check to see if the pattern has completely transferred. If it hasn't, re-flour the mold and try again on a new piece of dough. It may take several tries to get a clean impression. Cut out your piece with a cookie cutter or small knife. Remember that these pieces may be smaller and thinner than your roof or walls and will cook more quickly.

The wood grain impression mat can be easily removed from the dough if you bend the mat outward along the grain of the texture to create a taco shape (Fig. 10). This creates extra space between the long grain lines and releases the dough easily.

Fig. 9

Fig. 10

MODELING GINGERBREAD

Gingerbread dough can be modeled to form shapes such as the runners for the sleigh on page 65 and the stones on the bridge on page 61. Trace the shape of your item onto parchment paper, and mold on top of the outline. The bridge sides are simply small balls of dough laid closely together, baked, and glazed. Use a paintbrush and water to slightly dampen dough pieces meant to bake together. Snakes of dough form the sleigh runners.

After baking, three-dimensional items flatten on the cookie sheet side. Make certain that in making two of an object you make two mirror images—for example, a set of sleigh runners with the spiral to the right and a second set with the spiral to the left. The flat side of each will face inward.

Before you cement your four walls together, think carefully about the decorations and candies. I always decorate the four sides of a house before assembly. This is especially important if you plan to pipe icing designs. With the wall pieces lying flat, gravity works for you instead of against you. Let decorated pieces lie flat until the icing dries and hardens completely.

I find it easiest to decorate the roof panels after they're on the house. The projects in this book will specify whether you attach a bare roof to assembled sides or decorate the roof while it's still flat.

The one exception is when I make bare gingerbread houses for young children to decorate. Those houses must be fully assembled and completely dry before little hands work their magic. Many families with young children make gingerbread houses together every year. If this is the case, assemble your gingerbread house and have it completely dry before the decorating team arrives.

BUILDING THE HOUSE

Are your gingerbread cookies completely baked without a hint of softness or moisture? Have you finished any delicate icing work on the four walls and allowed it to dry? If so, it's time to build.

Ready for Assembly

Check each gingerbread piece against its pattern. If the edges don't align, they need to be trimmed. This is easier with warm gingerbread. Warm the cookie in the oven or microwave it for 10 seconds. Lay the pattern piece over the warm cookie and use a serrated knife to trim off excess with a light sawing motion. An alternative, especially with thinner brittle pieces, is to score the cookie with a serrated knife and snap off the excess.

Use a pastry brush or clean microfiber cloth to remove excess flour on the fronts or backs of the pieces. Hold the pieces up to one another and make certain that everything fits together.

Hidden Internal Supports

High relative humidity and temperature extremes can weaken gingerbread cookies, sometimes to the point of breaking. Consider adding additional internal supports if your house will be subjected to moisture, cold, or heat.

The internal support I find most helpful is a cube cut from rice cereal treats (Fig. 11). Ice a cereal treat cube into the inside corners of your house to help support the walls and keep the corner angles close to 90°.

Large houses may need extra roof support. Do this by making extra front and back house sections and icing them midway or at intervals inside the house (Fig. 12). If the entire gingerbread house must be edible, cut and bake gingerbread for the supports. If not, cut foam core or corrugated cardboard pieces. The internal supports must be

Fig. 11

Fig. 12

slightly narrower to fit inside the house because the house front and back are cemented onto the ends of the side walls. Trim ¾ inch off each side of an extra section so it will fit inside the house (Fig. 13).

Icing the Wrong Side to Increase Strength

Another option is to coat the wrong sides of the house with royal icing. This adds some support and prevents moisture soaking into the back of the cookies. Remember to ice the wrong sides before decorating the fronts. Spread a thin layer completely over the cookie (Fig. 14). Use a spatula to remove icing near the edges of the front and back panels and along the roof panel sides. This is where gingerbread joins gingerbread when you assemble the house and the extra icing would add bulk where it's not wanted. If your house has open windows, tint the interior icing brown to match the gingerbread's color.

Putting It All Together

All of the house patterns provided have parallel sides with the front and back iced onto the ends of the sides. When you look at the front of your house, the sides should not stick out. This house is joined with white icing to clearly show the positions of the walls (Fig. 15).

Make thick royal icing to use as cement. The icing alone should hold the house pieces upright and together. Because this icing holds the house together, use a liberal amount. Some icing will seep out around the edges, so tint it to match the color of the walls. I find that brown food coloring with a small touch of Egg Yellow most often matches the color of the gingerbread itself.

The color of the icing that cements the house to the base should be the same color as your ground cover.

Fig. 13

Fig. 14

Fig. 15

Raise the Walls

Mark the middle of the base with a pen or dot of icing. You may choose to center your house on the base or set it slightly back so that there is more front yard to decorate.

Lay plush cotton towels around the base. If you need to set a piece of gingerbread down, the towels will cushion the cookie and any dry royal icing decorations. Collect several cans of food, coffee cups, or jars that can support the house pieces.

Cover a can with a towel to provide padded support to the decorated side of the front wall.

Load a decorating bag with royal icing and a large open tip and cover it with a damp cloth.

Pipe a thick line of icing along the bottom edge of your front wall. Push the wall firmly onto the base and support it gently with one can on the inside (wrong side) and the padded can on the outside (decorated side). Check its position and make sure that it stands straight up (Fig. 16).

Fig. 17

Fig. 18

Fig. 16

Fig. 19

Pipe zigzags of icing on the wrong side of the house's front panel down the edges where both sides will attach (Fig. 17).

Pipe a thick line of icing along the bottom edge of a side wall.

Press the side wall down onto the base and sideways into the icing on the front wall. Check that the corner forms a right angle. Support the side wall with cans if necessary.

For larger houses, consider icing a rice cereal treat square inside the corner to reinforce it and help maintain a 90° angle. Repeat with the other side wall (Fig. 18).

Pipe a thick line of icing on the base where the back wall will sit. Pipe zigzags of brown icing on the wrong side of the house's front section down the edges where both sides will attach (Fig. 19).

Push the back wall firmly onto the base and into the sides. Check its position and that it stands straight up. Finesse the four walls into position with right angles at each corner (the rice cereal treat squares are a great help with this). Remove excess icing from the exterior joints with the tip of a butter knife or spatula. To reinforce the joints you may want to pipe icing zigzags back and forth along the inside of the corners (Fig. 20).

Pipe a large dab of brown icing somewhere on the base alongside the house. Use this spare blob of icing to test for dryness.

Fig. 20

Attach the Roof

Attach the roof panels, one at a time, only after the walls of the house are stable. Pipe a thick line or zigzags of royal icing along the top edge of the front and back wall panels (Fig. 21). Press one roof panel in place and hold it steady with your hands for 30 seconds. When you release the roof panel it should stay in place. If it slides, you'll need to add more powdered sugar to thicken the icing. Attach the second roof panel and hold both in place for another 30 seconds (Fig. 22). Pipe a line of icing along the top ridge of the roof to cement the two panels together.

Let everything dry completely and you will have a standing house.

Fig. 21

TIP: Some people use carmelized sugar to glue their gingerbread pieces together. The brown liquid sugar hardens to a lollipop-like state, but if you live in a humid area, the moisture in the air can cause the sugar to melt and run down the sides of your house.

HOW TO REPAIR A BROKEN PIECE

Don't panic if you accidentally break a piece of gingerbread. Many pieces can be repaired with royal icing and extra supports iced to the back. Glue a scrap cookie across the break with royal icing and let it dry overnight before assembly. If the support need not be edible, ice wooden chopsticks and lay them across the back of the

Fig. 22

Fig. 23

break (Fig. 23). Don't attempt this with roof panels, because the extra weight of the bracing can further stress an already fragile roof.

ASSEMBLING THE HOUSE SEPARATE FROM THE BASE

Assemble the house following the instructions above, but use a cookie sheet covered with waxed paper instead of the base. When dry, the waxed paper will easily peel away

Fig. 24

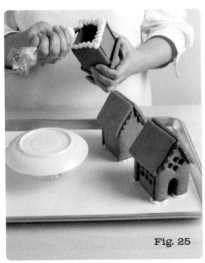
Fig. 25

when you transfer the house (Fig. 24).

Check that the four walls of your house are firmly iced together and the icing is dry. Attaching the roof and letting the house completely dry before transfer will make it even more robust. Pipe a thick rectangle of royal icing on the base where the house will rest. Gently lift the house with two hands, holding the front of it with one hand, and holding the back with the other. Press it firmly down into the icing.

Lift smaller houses up and pipe the white icing directly onto the bottom edges (Fig. 25).

Royal Icing

Before you cement your four walls together, think carefully about the decorations and candies. I always decorate the four sides of a house before assembly. This is especially important if you plan to pipe icing designs. With the wall pieces lying flat, gravity works for you instead of against you. Let decorated pieces lie flat until the icing dries and hardens completely.

Royal icing contains egg whites, powdered sugar, water, and flavoring.

Egg Whites

The egg whites can be fresh, fresh pasteurized, liquid pasteurized, dried, or meringue powder. Throughout my childhood we used fresh egg whites, and I still use them for houses that won't be eaten. Concerns about possible food poisoning from raw eggs have led me to try other recipes.

Meringue powder is powdered egg whites mixed with powdered sugar. Different brands of meringue powder can have different proportions of powdered egg whites; please read the recipe included with your particular container of meringue powder. The recipe below works well with several different brands.

The acidity of lemon juice or cream of tartar stabilizes the foam of whipped egg whites. You'll notice in the recipes below that you can use either. I prefer lemon juice because it's cheaper and the taste of lemon is undetectable in the finished icing.

Powdered Sugar

I buy powdered sugar the same way I buy produce—give it a good look and a squeeze to check for lumps. You can sift the powdered sugar to remove bigger lumps, but the tiny lumps remain and can be just as troublesome. Any small lump can clog a decorating tip, so if in doubt, sift the powdered sugar. On page 33, I'll show you how to filter out tiny lumps from thinned icing that you pipe through the tiniest of tips.

Flavorings

Flavoring your royal icing adds a wonderful smell and taste to the finished product. Wet royal icing smells like egg whites. Instead, enjoy the scent of peppermint or almond as your icing dries. Any clear extract can be used; vanilla and other colored extracts will color the icing. Oil-based flavors or emulsions, such as those used for candies, break down royal icing and can't be used.

EQUIPMENT

When it comes to gingerbread houses, you don't need a lot of fancy equipment to make and apply royal icing. You likely already have all or most of the components.

Powerful stand mixers easily whip up thick royal icing. If you use a handheld mixer, choose a bigger bowl or cut the recipe in half. Keeping a shallower layer of icing in the bowl will reduce wear on the mixer's motor. You can mix small amounts of royal icing in a teacup. Prepare for a workout, as you'll need to beat the egg whites and sugar for 5 to 10 minutes.

A dinner plate makes a fantastic resting place for the spatula. It contains the icing and speeds cleanup; just soak the plate and the icing dissolves.

Degrease with Vinegar

Equipment used to make and pipe royal icing must be completely free of grease. Even traces of grease can cause the egg white foam to break down. Mixing bowls, beaters, spatulas, knives, piping bags, and piping tips should be absolutely clean. Soap residue from incomplete rinsing or traces of grease on a silicone spatula can ruin your icing. Plastic, in particular, harbors unwanted grease. I degrease my equipment as an extra precaution. To do this, place your beater, spatula, and smaller storage cups inside the mixing bowl. Pour in some vinegar and swirl it all around. Rinse thoroughly and dry with a clean towel. This is especially helpful if you wish to store icing in sealed plastic bowls.

ROYAL ICING BEHAVIOR & TIPS

Egg white proteins do two things: They bind the sugar, and they form tiny air bubbles. The tiny bubbles increase the volume of royal icing to make it fluffier and easier to pipe.

Properly beaten royal icing will lose its translucency and become bright white, light, and slightly fluffy.

Beating the icing beyond this point will introduce more and larger air bubbles that make piping and

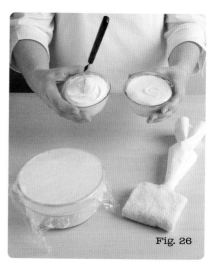

Fig. 26

flooding difficult. Use the slow speed on your mixer to reduce the number of large air bubbles. As an exception, I do sometimes overbeat icing to lighten it for covering large areas of landscaping. Landscaping icing doesn't support weight and the extra air bubbles speed drying.

Royal icing dries rock hard. That's why it makes such effective gingerbread cement! Cover bowls of icing with a damp cloth. A piping bag that sits unused for even a few minutes can form a crust over the end of the decorating tip. When I'm making icing, I dampen three clean cloths—one to cover the main bowl of icing, one to cover small cups of colored icing, and one to cover my piping bags.

Royal icing will keep in the refrigerator for several days to a week. Cover the bowl with a damp paper towel and then plastic wrap, and secure with a rubber band. Royal icing that sits for hours or is refrigerated can separate and will need to be beaten again.

Egg whites and meringue powder give royal icing strength and volume. Fresh egg whites make stronger icing but with less volume (air), while meringue powder makes icing with more volume but not as much strength. To maximize the benefits of both, I often use the meringue powder recipe but substitute fresh egg white for half of the water.

Dissolve the meringue powder in the water and add the fresh egg white(s). Beat until the powder is completely dissolved, then add powdered sugar. This is particularly helpful when piping fine lines.

Drying times vary greatly with relative humidity. Icing piped on a rainy day may need twelve hours to dry, instead of the three required on a cold, dry day. Drop several small blobs of icing on a small dish. You can poke and prod these to estimate when the icing on your project should be dry. If in doubt, wait! Think of the time you've spent creating your masterpiece. Continuing before the icing is dry could put your entire project in peril! Consider using a fan to increase the airflow over the damp icing.

ROYAL ICING RECIPES

Construction icing must be thick enough to hold the gingerbread pieces together, yet still fluid enough to travel through a piping bag. See the section on consistencies of royal icing for more information. The recipes below are for thick, stable, construction-grade royal icing.

ROYAL ICING WITH MERINGUE POWDER

This is my favorite gingerbread icing. It dries and handles well at all consistencies.

5 tablespoons meringue powder
½ to ⅔ cup water (4+ ounces)
1 tablespoon lemon juice (added for the acidity, taste will be unnoticeable) or 1 teaspoon cream of tartar
2 pound bag of powdered sugar (approximately 8 cups)
2 teaspoons peppermint extract or other flavored extract (no oil-based flavorings, only extracts)

Combine the meringue powder, water, and lemon juice (or cream of tartar). Mix until the meringue powder dissolves completely. Gradually add the powdered sugar on slow speed.

Beat the icing on medium speed for 2–4 minutes, scraping the sides occasionally until the icing is bright white, light, and fluffy. Add extract. Cover with a damp cloth.

ROYAL ICING WITH EGG WHITES (CAN BE PASTEURIZED)

Icing made with pasteurized egg whites is safe to eat but won't beat up to the same fluffy state that fresh egg whites create.

½ cup + 2 tablespoons liquid egg whites (5 ounces)
1 tablespoon lemon juice or 1 teaspoon of cream of tartar
8 cups powdered sugar (2 pounds)
2 teaspoons peppermint extract or other flavored extract (no oil-based flavorings, only extracts)

Beat eggs whites until frothy. Add the lemon juice (or cream of tartar). Set your mixer on slow speed and gradually add the powdered sugar.

Beat the icing on medium speed for 2–4 minutes, scraping the sides occasionally until bright white, light, and fluffy.

Add extract. Cover with a damp cloth.

ROYAL ICING CONSISTENCIES

Different decorations require different icing consistencies. Piping icing of the correct consistency is a delight. Icing that's too thick or too thin simply doesn't work. Time spent adjusting the consistency pays off.

In general, to make icing more stiff, add powdered sugar. To thin it, add water. Even a few drops of liquid can drastically alter your icing. I use a tablespoon, a teaspoon, and then an eyedropper to add water drop by drop.

When royal icing sits idle for more than 30 minutes, the air bubbles in it break down and it needs to be beaten again before use.

Thick Royal Icing

Use thick icing to cement walls together, attach roofs and chimneys, and anchor the gingerbread house to its base. This icing must be thick enough to hold cookies together yet thin enough to squeeze through a piping bag. Stick a spatula into thick icing and it should remain standing (Fig. 27). When I first started making gingerbread houses, I would test my icing by joining two squares of corrugated cardboard. Could I pipe it easily? Did it hold the cardboard pieces together? Would it hold heavier gingerbread pieces?

Medium Thick Royal Icing

Piping stars, trees, wreaths, stockings, fireplaces, and much more is done with royal icing of a medium thick consistency. It should hold its shape, but it doesn't need to function as cement. Add water slowly, several drops or teaspoons at a time (depending on the amount of icing to be thinned). Use a butter knife to make peaks with the icing. The top of each peak may lean over, but the peak itself should remain in place with a crisp shape. If the icing is too thin, you'll notice that the entire peak sags or the ridges gradually melt away (Fig. 28).

Medium Thin Royal Icing

Lines or scrolls piped with a fine tip require thinner icing. Icicles hanging from house eaves look especially realistic when made with medium thin icing. I make small amounts of medium thin icing in a coffee cup adding water drop by drop. Medium thin royal icing should flow easily from your decorating tip. Make a peak in the icing and it will remain a peak, but the peak will sag. If the peak disappears, the icing is too thin. I spend the most time adjusting consistency with medium thin icing. To test it, put a dollop inside your decorating tip and push it through with a finger. The icing that comes out should move easily, yet keep its defined shape. If the lines melt, it's too thin. If the lines crack or break, it's too thick.

FLOOD ICING

Flood icing is the consistency of syrup or honey. It flows to fill up a given area and dries to a shiny, smooth surface. To thin one cup of icing for flooding start by adding a single teaspoon of water and then

Fig. 27

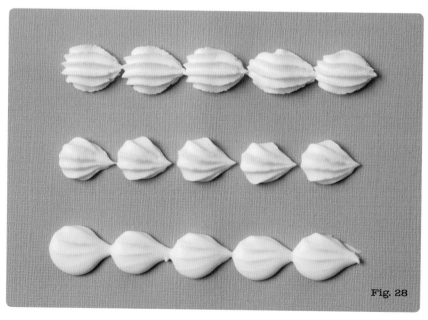

Fig. 28

Fig. 29

Fig. 30

proceed slowly adding water, drop by drop. To test it, lift up some icing with a knife and let it drip back into the bowl (Fig. 29). You have achieved a good flood consistency when the dripped icing disappears into the icing around it in about 10 seconds (Fig. 30). In Fig. 31 the flood icing in the center is a good consistency. The icing to the right is too stiff and the icing to the left is too loose.

COLORING ROYAL ICING

Tint icing any color of the rainbow using either paste or gel food coloring. Liquid food coloring adds too much water to the icing and shouldn't be used. Grocery stores and hobby stores sell several reliable brands of paste and gel colors.

Put a small amount of icing in a coffee or teacup. I find that cups with a rounded, bowl-like bottom work best. Add the coloring slowly in minute amounts. Paste colors can be added in small amounts using a toothpick; add gel colors drop by drop.

The colors in wet royal icing deepen with time and will dry to a darker hue. This can be handy when trying to achieve a rich, deep red or Christmas green. Color the icing and let it sit for at least 45 minutes, until its full color develops. One easy way to gauge the color is by looking at your spatula plate. The stray bits of royal icing left there will dry first.

Fig. 31

Piping Icing

Dots, teardrops, and simple flowers are all within reach of a beginning decorator. Connecting dots, shells, or teardrops in a line generates beautiful borders. Dots or stars arranged in a circle form simple flowers. Start with the simplest forms and advance to those that require more skill. There are practice templates at the back of the book. Practice will dramatically improve your piping and give you more confidence as you work on your house.

TIP: Cut a front and back to your house from colored paper and practice piping the exact design for your house. If you don't like it, throw it away and try again (Fig. 32)!

Getting the icing to the right consistency is key. The royal icing recipe will give you thick royal icing. You'll almost always adjust the consistency by adding water. Use small bowls, teacups, or coffee cups to thin and color small amounts of icing.

DECORATING TIPS

You can pipe a large number of items from a decorating bag and only one round tip. You can double this if you add a star tip to your collection. If you use paper cornets or disposable plastic piping bags, create a round tip just by slicing a small bit off the end.

These are the tips I find most useful for piping. Numbers stamped on the tips' sides identify them.

✦ Round opening No. 00–No. 12: size increases as number increases (Fig. 33)
  • No. 0: extremely small round opening for fine piping
  • No. 3: very small round opening for piping
  • No. 5: round opening medium
  • No. 10: round opening large
✦ Star opening No. 13–No. 22: size increases as number increases (Fig. 34)
✦ Any of the star tips, one smaller and one larger

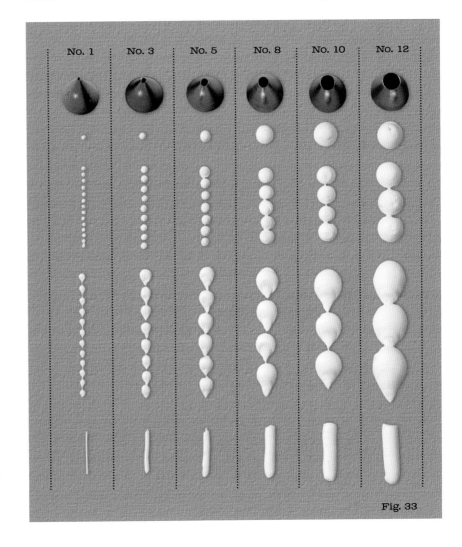

Fig. 33

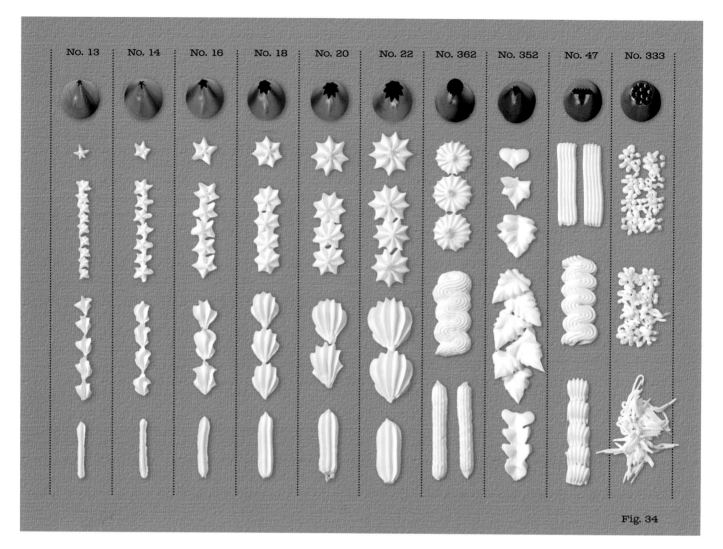

NO. 13   NO. 14   NO. 16   NO. 18   NO. 20   NO. 22   NO. 362   NO. 352   NO. 47   NO. 333

Fig. 34

✦ Other nice decorating tips to have (Fig. 34):
- No. 46 or No.47 flat on one side, ridges on the other
- No. 349 or No. 352 leaf tip
- No. 233/234 grass tip

Couplers

A coupler is a two-piece plastic adapter that makes it possible to change decorating tips without taking the icing out of the bag. Drop the cone-shaped piece into the decorating bag, guide it down to the end, and snip the tip of the bag away. Add the tip to the outside of the bag and screw the ring of the coupler over it. To change a tip, simply unscrew the plastic ring.

CHOOSING A DECORATING BAG

Disposable plastic bags, parchment paper cornets, and reusable featherweight bags are all available.

Featherweight bags are made from plastic-coated polyester cloth. You can wash and reuse them hundreds of times. Featherweight bags come in several sizes. Use small bags for small amounts of icing and for fine piping. Use larger bags for the larger amounts of icing needed on roofs or for ground cover. Handling a bag is easiest when it's no more than half full of icing.

It's important that no other icing be used in bags that will hold royal icing, because even a minute amount of buttercream residue can break down the royal icing.

Disposable plastic decorating bags are used once and discarded after removing the coupler and tip. Many of these bags have ridges along the sides where the two pieces of plastic weld together. Turn the disposable bags inside out so this ridge doesn't chafe against your hands. Trim the top off of disposable bags if you need to make them smaller and more maneuverable.

Parchment cornets are made from rolled or sheet parchment paper. Making the bags is quite straightforward; however, I find them more difficult to manage while decorating. If you haven't decorated with icing in a bag before, disposable plastic or reusable bags are well worth the money and convenience.

Making Parchment Cornets

1. Cut a right triangle of parchment paper and place it with the 90° angle toward you and the hypotenuse away from you. For ease of explanation, I've labeled the corners A, B, and C (Fig. 35).

2. Take the top left corner (A) and roll it toward you (Fig. 36). The corner will end up inverted and aligned within the bottom 90° angle (C). Hold it in place there and you will see a conic shape (Fig. 37).

3. Take the top right corner (B). Roll it down over the cone and around the back until that corner is also aligned within the bottom 90° angle (C) (Fig 38). I pick up the cornet as I'm doing this.

4. Adjust the points of the three corners so that the tip of the cornet is completely closed. (Fig 39).

5. Fold the corners into the cone and press to make a crease. Tear a small section and fold this in again to secure the fold (Fig 40).

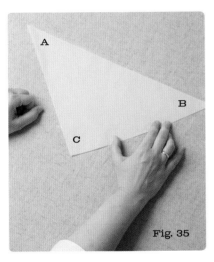
Fig. 35

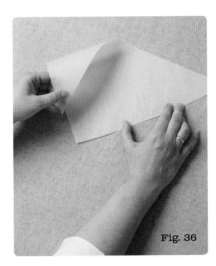
Fig. 36

Fig. 37

Fig. 38

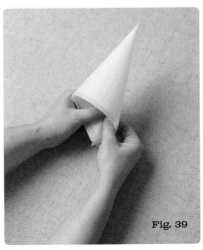
Fig. 39

Fig. 40

PREPARING A PIPING BAG

New piping bags must have an opening cut so that the coupler or tip pokes out. Trim conservatively; if the opening is too large, the icing will push the tip or coupler out the end of the bag. Note that the coupler and tip are different sizes. If the end is clipped to hold a coupler, the opening is much too large to use with a tip alone.

Drop in the tip and let it fall to the end of the bag. If the entire metal opening of the tip is not exposed (where the icing will extrude), remove the tip and clip very small slivers off of the bag's end until it fits (Fig. 41).

If you are using a coupler, remove the coupler's outer ring and drop the cone-shaped section into the bag. Push it down to the very end. Mark where the coupler's first screw thread hits. Remove the coupler and trim the bag to your mark. Trim in small increments; you can always trim more. Test the coupler again and make certain that two screw threads are exposed.

Parchment cornets are often used without tips—merely snip off a small bit from the end—but decorating tips can also be added in the same way you would with a reusable bag.

PIPING WITH MEDIUM THIN ROYAL ICING

Lines, dots, hearts, and scrolls piped with a fine tip require thinner icing. Medium thin royal icing should flow easily from your decorating tip when you apply a small amount of pressure. Make a peak in the icing and it will remain a peak but the peak will sag. If the peak disappears, the icing is too thin.

Fig. 41

PIPING WITH MEDIUM THICK ROYAL ICING

Stars, flowers, trees, leaves, and large dots are all piped with icing of a medium thick consistency. When you lift a bit of icing with the spatula, it should form a soft peak with a tip that leans over.

FILLING & USING A PIPING BAG

Remove the coupler's outer ring and drop the coupler into the bag. Add the tip and secure it by screwing on the outer ring.

Fold down the top 2 inches of the bag to keep them free of icing.

While holding the bag in one hand, take a spoonful of icing with the other and put into the bag. Use your bag-holding hand to grab onto

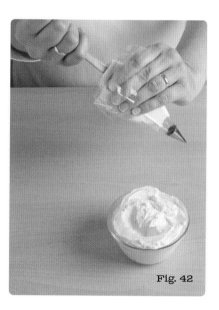

Fig. 42

the spoon inside while pulling the spoon out (Fig. 42). Decorating bags handle easily if you fill them no more than halfway. Squeezing the bag in the palm of your hand controls the flow of icing, so imagine a glop of icing the size of your palm.

Twist the bag as you would a bread bag to close the top. Rubber bands can secure the twist and prevent icing from backing out the top of the bag.

Cover the filled tubes with a slightly damp cloth to keep the icing in the tip from drying.

HOLDING THE BAG

Lay the bag across the palm of your hand with the twisted end coming out between your thumb and forefinger. Use the thumb and finger to tightly grip the twist of the bag and keep the icing headed down toward the bag's tip. Squeeze your hand with all four fingers to apply pressure and force the icing out.

PIPING

Piping follows a basic pattern.

1. Hold the piping bag with the decorating tip pointing to the surface.
2. Gently touch the tip to the surface.
3. Squeeze to start the flow of icing while raising the tip just slightly above the surface. The icing attaches to your touch point.
4. Use varying amounts of motion and pressure to create the shapes you want.
5. Stop squeezing the bag to stop the icing.
6. Pull the tip away.

Some forms are piped with the bag straight up above the surface at 90°, while others require holding the bag at a 45° angle.

These things are key to piping:

✦ Icing of the correct consistency
✦ A smaller piping bag no more

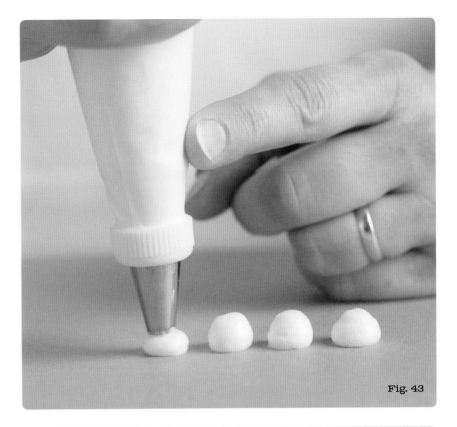

Fig. 43

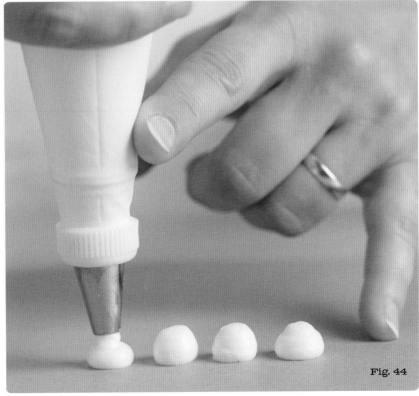

Fig. 44

than half filled with icing

♦ A flat surface

♦ Patience, practice, and steady hands!

You'll find that using one hand to squeeze the icing bag and the other hand to guide and support the tip will make your piping more steady and uniform. Leaving elbows or extra fingers on the work surface stabilizes your hands (Fig. 43 and 44).

The Dot

Use a round tip with medium thick or medium thin icing.

Holding the piping bag straight up at 90°, touch the tip to the surface and squeeze. While keeping the tip inside the dot, continue squeezing and lift the bag slightly (Fig. 43). When the dot is big enough, stop squeezing. Lift the tip clear. If you have a stray "tail" from the top of your dot, try using the tip to scrape it off as you finish or pat it down with a dry fingertip.

The Line

Choose a round tip to use with medium thin icing.

Hold the piping bag at 45°. Touch the tip gently to the surface and squeeze. Lift the tip slightly above the surface, continue squeezing, and pull gently down the line. The icing will fall from the tip with a slight arc (Fig. 45). Lay the icing down rather than "drawing" with it. Imagine the icing is a long

floppy spaghetti noodle and you're coaxing it down in a straight line.

When the line is done, stop squeezing and touch the tip to the surface to anchor the line. Lift the tip away.

The Teardrop or Shell

Choose a round or star tip. The teardrop shape is just a dot or star with the tail pulled out.

Touch the tip gently to the surface and squeeze while holding the piping bag at 45°. Lift the tip slightly and continue squeezing to increase the size of the dot then pull slowly away to make the tail (Fig. 46). Stop squeezing. This shape may work better if you slightly drag or scrape your tip on the surface at the tail's end.

The Heart

Pipe two teardrops next to each other with the points joining (Fig. 47).

The Zigzag

Choose a round or star tip to use with medium thick icing.

Touch the tip gently to the surface and squeeze while holding the piping bag at 45°. Lift the tip slightly and continue squeezing while you move back and forth, laying the string of icing up and down (Fig. 48). Touch the tip to the surface and stop squeezing at the end of the zigzag and pull away.

The Star

Choose a star tip to use with medium thick icing.

Touch the tip gently to the surface and squeeze while holding the piping bag straight up at 90°. Lift the tip slightly above the surface and continue squeezing until the star is the right size (Fig. 49). Stop squeezing and lift the tip away.

The Rosette

Choose a star tip to use with medium thick icing. Touch the tip gently to the surface and squeeze while holding the piping bag straight up at 90°. Lift the tip slightly above the surface and continue squeezing while you drop a circle of icing around the start point (Fig. 50). Stop squeezing and pull away in the direction of your circle instead of straight up. This will leave a small tail instead of a blunt stopping point. For a wreath, pipe a bigger circle to make an open rosette.

Leaves

Pipe a teardrop for a simple leaf. To give the teardrop a larger base, zigzag slightly as you begin. Piping a teardrop shape with tip No. 349 or No. 352 creates leaves that are more three-dimensional. These tips resemble the open mouth of a baby bird. As you pipe leaves, keep the points of the tips up and down, just like a bird's beak opens. Using medium thick icing, touch one point of the tip gently to the surface and

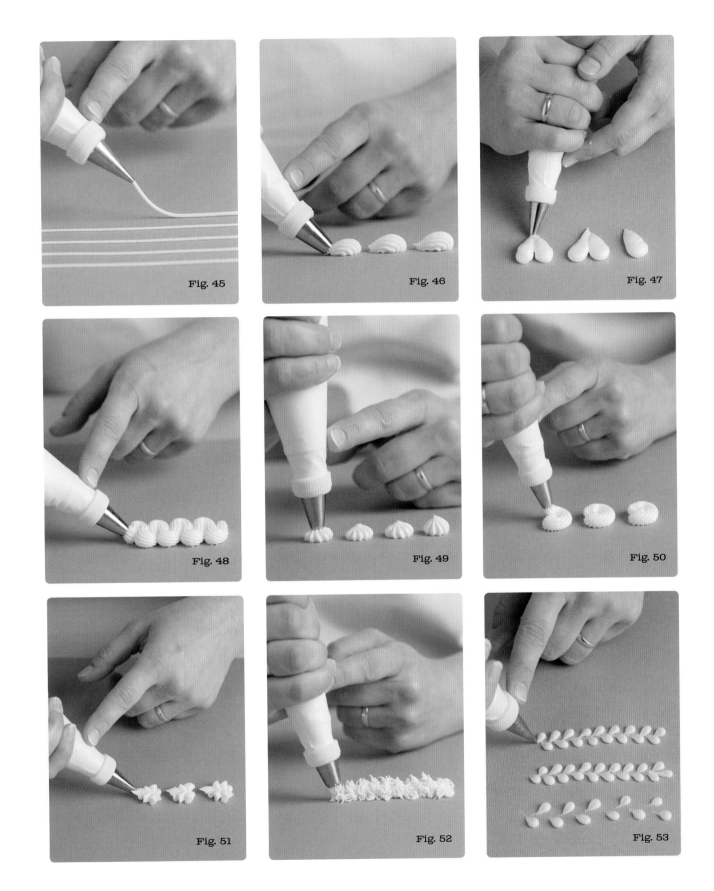

Fig. 45

Fig. 46

Fig. 47

Fig. 48

Fig. 49

Fig. 50

Fig. 51

Fig. 52

Fig. 53

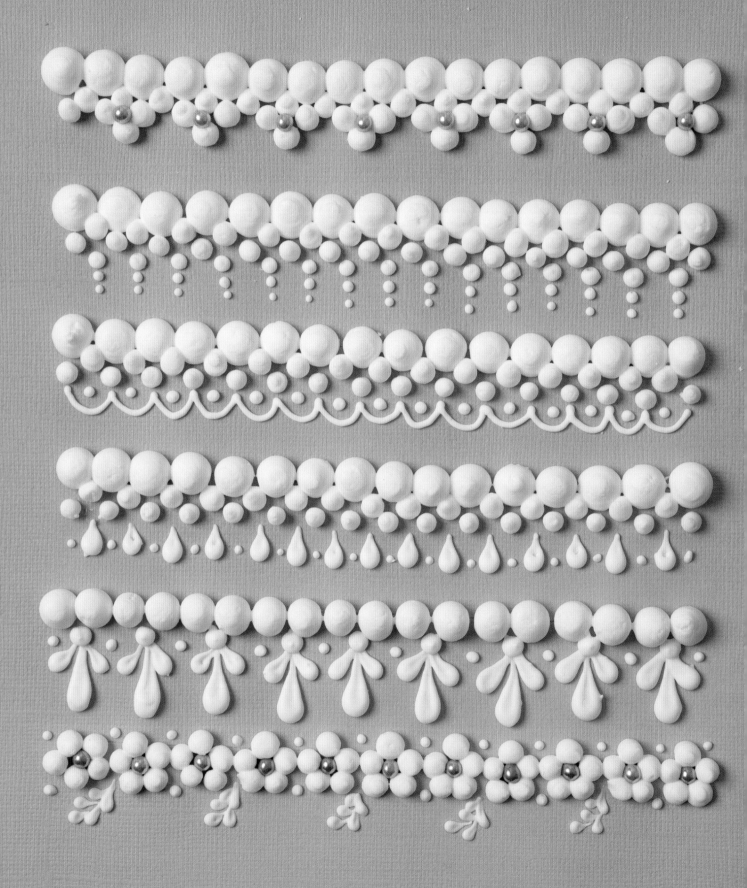

squeeze. Continue squeezing until your leaf is the correct size, then pull away as you stop squeezing (Fig. 51). If the leaf's tip breaks short, use your fingers to gently pull it out to a point. To vary the base of the leaf, zigzag slightly or use a pumping motion to create pressure waves.

Grass

Using tip No. 233 and medium thick icing, hold the icing bag straight up at 90°. Hold the end of the tip just barely above the surface and squeeze to attach. Continue to squeeze and lift up slightly to produce the length of grass needed (Fig. 52). It's important to attach the strands of icing to the surface before lifting or the entire clump of grass will come up on your tip.

THE FINE PRINT OF FINE PIPING

When using small (No. 1, No. 0, No. 00) tips, even tiny clumps of sugar can cause difficulties. Royal icing piped through tips with very small openings requires special treatment.

Mix the icing at slow speed to reduce the size and number of air bubbles; a bubble causes the line of icing to break as it comes through the tip. If you find bubbles, gently work the icing back and forth against the side of the bowl with a spatula like an artist works paint with a palette knife. This removes some of the air.

Thin a coffee cup full of icing just a bit. Pipe a few teardrops to test the consistency. The icing should flow easily from the tube and maintain its teardrop shape without flattening completely.

Even tiny lumps of powdered sugar or meringue powder can clog the fine tip openings. Strain thinned royal icing to remove any lumps. Cut a 6 inch square from a new, inexpensive pair of pantyhose. Secure the hose loosely over the top of a coffee cup with a rubber band. Spoon the icing into the middle of the hose. Carefully remove the rubber band and gather and twist the hose edges to form a small sack of icing (Fig. 54). Continue to twist and push the icing until it squeezes out of the hose and drops into the cup (Fig. 55). Voila, no lumps!

Use a small round tip on your decorating bag and fill it only one third full. See the photos in the piping section for suggestions on

how to support and steady your hands. Practice, practice, practice. With the correct equipment and icing of the proper consistency, practice can make fine piping a joy.

Vines

Make a vine by piping angled teardrops (Fig. 53).

Curlicues, Scrolls, & Spirals

Pipe these freehand or use the patterns on page 129 to practice. Photocopy the pattern, tape it to the table, tape waxed paper on top, and pipe away. Squeeze harder or slow the movement of your tip to make the lines thicker. Use less pressure or move more quickly for thinner lines. Try for fluid movement. Keep the tip quite close to the surface and let the icing build rather than drop. When you pressure pipe, you force the icing to build in certain areas by slowing or stopping the movement of the tip.

Fig. 54

Fig. 55

Part Two

The
Projects

Haunted Hideaway

Halloween is the perfect time to warm the cool fall air with gingerbread straight from the oven. The orange windows of the Haunted Hideaway glow like the face of a friendly jack-o-lantern. For a spookier look, cut the pointed windows askew and attach the shutters haphazardly.

TIME-SAVERS

- Add battery-operated tea lights around the house instead of lighting it from within.
- Leave the windows open without adding the sheet gelatin. The light will shine out in its true color.
- Don't cut windows or light the house at all. Bake solid walls with no windows. When cool, pipe windows with orange or yellow royal icing.
- Ice the roof solid orange and decorate with Halloween sprinkles.
- Use mellowcreme or gumdrop pumpkins instead of molding them from fondant.
- Use a smaller base and surround the house only with candies.
- Omit the topiaries, hay bales, and ghost. Add lots of pretty candy to fill the space.

LARGE HAUNTED HIDEAWAY

You can make a Halloween gingerbread house of any size. The large house is about 223 mm tall, the medium house is about 110 mm tall, and the small house is about 75 mm tall.

The Pattern

Enlarge the Halloween House pattern to 140% and cut out the pattern pieces including the door and Haunted Hideaway small and large windows.

Bake the House

Make two recipes of Construction-Grade Gingerbread dough (page 9). Use dark unsulfured molasses as the sole liquid sweetener (1 cup of molasses, no corn syrup or honey). Add black food coloring to achieve a dark black dough. Roll the dough ¼–⅜ inch thick on parchment paper. Cut out two front/back pieces, two sides, and two roof panels. Remove the dough scraps, cut the parchment paper to separate the cookies, and transfer them to cool baking sheets.

Freeze the unbaked front, back, and side panels for 20 minutes to stiffen the dough. Cold dough resists deformation and allows easier and more intricate cuts. Cut out a front door, front and side windows, and the back access port (for the battery-

Fig. 1

operated tea lights) with a clean craft knife (Fig. 1). Save the door and use a small square Kemper cutter to cut four windows in it. If you don't have a cutter use the end of a drinking straw or large round piping tip to cut holes. Smooth any rough edges with your fingers.

Bake at 325°F for 15–25 minutes, until firm. Check for firmness when cool. Re-bake if necessary until hard.

Tinting fondant, pastillage, and icing to a deep black hue requires a good amount of food coloring. It's much easier to purchase fondant that is pre-colored black or red if you want to use those colors. Black and red food coloring can stain your hands and work surface. Keep the food coloring bottles and icing utensils resting on a plate and wear disposable gloves to keep your hands clean.

Roll pre-tinted black fondant and texture it with a roller or mat. Cut two pairs of large front shutters, four pairs of small front shutters, and two pairs of rectangular side shutters. Allow the fondant to dry. Add black luster dust and silver disco dust (Fig. 2).

Place the front, back, and sides wrong side up. Cut pieces of sheet gelatin (or colored cellophane) that are roughly ½ inch larger on all sides than each window opening. Outline each window (on the wrong side

Fig. 2

of the gingerbread) with black or orange royal icing ¼ inch from the edge. Place the piece of gelatin over the window and gently press it into the icing (Fig. 3). Watch that royal icing doesn't squeeze out into the window panel, where it will show. Using a pastry paintbrush, paint the gelatin pieces with orange food coloring and allow them to dry. You can thin the food coloring with a drop of water if necessary.

When the gelatin is dry, turn the pieces right side up. Attach shutters

Fig. 3

with black royal icing and allow them to dry for at least 10 minutes.

Assemble the four walls of the house using the instructions on page 15 with thick black royal icing.

Decorate the Roof

Fit a piping bag with a No. 3 round tip and add ⅓ cup medium thick orange royal icing. Outline each roof panel.

Thin 1½ cup orange royal icing to flood consistency (see Flood Icing, page 22).

Thin ½ cup black royal icing to a thicker flood consistency. Ideally, disturbances will disappear, leaving a smooth surface after 14 seconds. Fit a piping bag with a small round tip. Stand the bag up vertically in a cup or glass with the tip resting at the bottom. Fold the edges of the bag back and pour in the black icing.

Flood one roof panel with orange icing. With the black icing, immediately pipe several sets of concentric circles that start small and become larger. Rest the piping bag back in the glass. Put the tip of a toothpick in the center of a set of circles and draw it outward past the edge of the largest circle (Fig. 4). Repeat around the circles until your spiderwebs are complete. When the first roof panel is finished, flood the second with orange icing and weave your webs. Allow the panels to remain flat as they dry. A fan speeds the process.

Fig. 4

When the roof is completely dry, lay a line of icing up and down the top edges of the house front and back. Press one roof panel into place and then the other. Hold for 60 seconds to make certain they're set. Add a line of icing where the roof panels meet.

More Decorating

Pipe a border around the roof using tip No. 18 with medium thick black icing. Pipe larger zigzags along the ridge of the roof and decorate with black jellybeans and orange chocolate balls.

Chop and color one bag of unsweetened coconut (see Coconut as Ground Cover, page 89). Color 2 cups of royal icing green and spread a thin layer over the base. The remaining icing is for borders and trees. Press the coconut firmly into the icing to thoroughly embed the particles (see instructions on page 89). Brush off any extra coconut. It's important to remove all loose coconut so that the candies you add will stick to the base.

Use a toothpick to mark the front walkway area. Scrape any green icing and coconut away. Cover the walkway with black icing and press in poppy seeds.

Attach the door in a slightly open position with black royal icing. Attach a doorknob, such as a bone-shaped candy.

Use the green royal icing to pipe walkway borders and push in candies, such as candy corn, gumballs, and black jellybeans.

Pipe green icing around the base of the house and attach candies around the base. The house pictured has gumdrops and fruit slices.

Construct hay bales from brick-shaped pieces of rice cereal treats. Stick a toothpick into the bottom center of each. Make hay-colored icing with a small amount of brown food coloring and a very small amount of Egg Yellow. Hold the toothpick and bale in your left hand while you pipe icing through tip No. 233/234 along the length of the bale. Make short stubby "grass" on the ends of the bale. Place the toothpick into Styrofoam to keep the hale bale upright until dry. Add other decorations and candies.

+ Mellowcreme pumpkins or pumpkins modeled from fondant
+ Ghosts constructed from shaped rice cereal treats and covered with white fondant. Make eyes by cutting tiny circles from black fondant with the small end of decorating tip No. 8. Affix with edible glue (page 10). You can also draw the eyes on with black edible markers.
+ Black cats or bats from black fondant
+ Fondant flowerpots and trees for topiaries

✦ Add a border around the base of the house with tip No. 18 and add sprinkles.

Light the House

Create a strip of battery-operated tea lights (see Method 1 in the Interior Lighting section, page 96). Insert the strip of electric tea lights through the back access port (see full-page photo).

MEDIUM HAUNTED HIDEAWAY

Follow the flow of the directions for the Large Haunted Hideaway with the following changes.

✦ Decrease the Halloween House pattern to 70%.

✦ Cut windows in the back instead of an access port. Cut a front door and a window in each side.

✦ Do not attach the house to the base if you want to light it. Instead, assemble the house on waxed paper. Attach roof panels, candies along the roof ridge, roof trim, and the door. Let everything dry thoroughly. Peel the house off of the waxed paper and inspect the interior to make certain icing has securely joined all the pieces. If not, pipe extra black icing along the seams inside the house or outside. Candy corn or other flat candies can be cemented to the house sides with black icing (Fig. 5).

✦ Completely cover the base with

Fig. 5

green icing and coconut and add the walkway. Gently place the dried house in the center of the base. Add trim, trees, or candies anywhere except where they touch the house (Fig. 6).

✦ Lift the house up to turn on the battery-powered tea light.

SMALL HAUNTED HIDEAWAY

Follow the flow of the directions for the Medium Haunted Hideaway but decrease the Halloween House pattern to 50%.

Fig. 6

The contrast between the deep, warm, red background and cool, white piping give this house its charm. See the patterns on pages 128-130 for details of the piping. Practice on waxed paper before you pipe on the house itself. Better yet, use your house pattern to cut pieces from dark paper and practice piping white details on paper the exact size of your house. You'll find that using a fan will drastically reduce the time it takes for this house to dry.

TIME-SAVERS

- Use a fan to reduce drying time, especially with red flood icing.
- Omit the candy cane chimney and enjoy a pure white, sparkling roof.
- Use a smaller base and surround the house with candies instead of piping sugar cone trees.
- Omit the lake. Use candy rocks instead of making rocks with fondant.
- Use white candies to decorate the red house instead of piping the intricate patterns. The contrast of white on red will give much the same look.

LARGE KARI'S SKI CABIN

The pattern pieces also contain the piping templates. When you've enlarged or decreased the pattern, pipe directly on it for practice. The large house is about 273 mm tall, the medium house is about 110 mm tall, and the small house is about 80 mm tall.

The Pattern

Enlarge the Kari's Ski Cabin pattern to 140% and cut out the pieces including the door and windows.

Make the Pastillage Items

Whether you use pastillage or fondant, create these first so they can dry.

WINDOWS, SHUTTERS, & DOOR

Roll blue fondant or pastillage ⅓–½ inch thick. Cut three large and two small windows.

Roll white fondant or pastillage ½ inch thick and cut a door. Use your fingers to smooth and round the edges.

Roll white fondant or pastillage ⅓ inch thick, then emboss it with a wood grain mat (see Embossing Fondant or Pastillage, page 80). You'll need to roll out several

Fig. 1

43

sections of fondant to make all of the shutters. Cut out three large right shutters, three large left shutters, two small right shutters, and two small left shutters (Fig. 1).

Put all of these on waxed paper and set them aside to dry.

ROCKS

If chocolate or jellybean rocks are unavailable, use fondant to create several small rocks to go around the pond (see Rocks, page 94).

Pipe the Sugar Cone Trees and Wreath

Create trees in white and light blue by piping large teardrops of royal icing onto sugar cones (see Sugar Cone Trees, page 90). Vary the height of the trees by starting the bottom row of teardrops at different points along the length of the cone. Sprinkle the trees with sanding sugar or edible glitter as you pipe.

Create small green, white, and blue snowman trees of varying heights (see Piping Trees as Royal Icing Transfers, page 91) with tips No. 10 and No. 8.

Pipe several small, tall stars for tiny evergreens along the lake.

Pipe a green wreath with tip #20. Later, when you cover the four walls with red icing, pipe red berries on the wreath with a No. 3 tip.

Create the Chimney

Unwrapped candy canes, lollipops, and other hard candies absorb

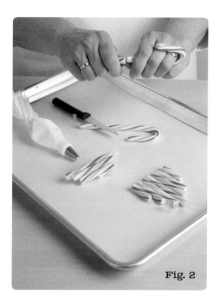

Fig. 2

moisture from the air and become liquid. They will drip down your house and pool on the base. If you live in a humid area you have three options for the chimney: Leave the candy canes wrapped (if there's no chance they will be eaten with the wrapper on), create canes from fondant (see Making Fondant Candy Canes, page 82), or simply omit the chimney altogether and enjoy an uninterrupted, sparkling, elegant roof.

Score then break the straight ends of candy canes to make a set of canes like those in Fig. 2. Join the canes with royal icing in a stair-step fashion with the original ends level and the broken ends staggered. If you have left the candy canes wrapped in cellophane, cover the broken ends with royal icing to seal them from the air (the rest of the cane is protected by cellophane).

Fig. 3

Bake the House

Make two recipes of Construction-Grade Gingerbread dough (page 9). Roll the dough ¼–⅜ inch thick on parchment paper. Cut out two house front/back pieces, two sides, and two roof panels. Remove the extra dough and trim the parchment around each cookie. Transfer the parchment-backed cookies to cool baking sheets.

Bake at 350°F for about 20 minutes, until firm. Allow the cookies to cool and check to make certain they're firm and tough. Re-bake if necessary at 275°F until hard.

Paint the House Red

The four walls of this house are outlined and flooded with red royal icing. Review the instructions for Flood Icing on page 84.

Color 4 cups of royal icing red with gel or paste food coloring. Red food coloring can stain your hands and work surface. Keep the food coloring bottles and icing utensils resting on a plate and wear disposable gloves to keep your hands unstained.

Be aware, tinting icing to a deep red hue requires a good amount of food coloring. When you achieve a bright red hue, stop adding food coloring. Cover the icing with a damp cloth and let it sit for an hour. The color will darken over this time. Remember that as it dries the color will darken even more. To test the final color, put a small dab of icing on a plate and let it dry. Fig. 3 shows the same red icing wet (left) and dry (right). Add more food coloring if necessary.

Lay the front, back, and two side panels right side up. Pipe an outline around each cookie with red medium thick royal icing and a No. 3 round tip. Except at the beginning and end of the border, keep your decorating tip just above the surface of the cookie. Lay the line of icing down in a single solid line. Repair any holes or breaks (see Flood Icing, page 84). By the time you've outlined the last cookie, the first should be ready to flood.

Remove 1 cup of red icing and set it aside for later. Thin the remaining red icing to flood consistency. Drop spoonfuls of icing onto a cookie beginning near the outline and finishing in the middle (Fig. 4). Shake the cookie gently to help settle the icing. Pop any air bubbles with a pin. Allow these to dry completely—this could take 24 hours. If desired, use a fan to speed this up. If the red icing isn't completely dry, it will bleed into the white piping you're going to add.

Decorate the Four Walls

Paint the door with edible glue (page 10), piping gel, or a thin layer of icing. Dip it in coarse sugar crystals or sanding sugar to add sparkle (Fig. 5). Attach a heart-shaped sprinkle and a dragée doorknob.

Fig. 4

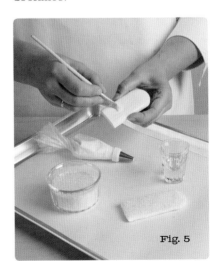

Fig. 5

Use white icing to attach the door. Attach the large central window, then the two smaller windows on either side of the door. Attach the shutters next to each window. Attach a large blue window and shutters in the middle of each side wall (Fig. 6).

Attach the wreath above the front middle window.

Pipe the White Decorations

It's time to pipe the white icing. Look at the patterns on pages 128–130 for details of the piping. Check out the entire Piping section (page 25), especially the Fine Print of Fine Piping (page 33).

Practice piping elsewhere before you pipe on your house. Photocopy the pattern, tape it to the table, tape waxed paper on top and practice piping directly over the design. Use your house pattern to cut pieces from dark paper to practice piping white details on paper the exact size of your house. The Piping section shows different ways to support and steady your hands. Practice, practice, practice. Pipe the large dots first, then move on to the smaller dots, which are made with thinner icing.

Start with medium thick white royal icing and a No. 8 round tip. Fill the decorating bag only one third full to make it easier to handle.

Decorate the Front and Sides

First decorate the front and sides of the house. Put each cookie on a clean cloth so you can spin them easily and decorate from different angles. Leave the back panel to do last.

Pipe dots at the top and bottom of each window (Fig. 7). Use more pressure to increase the size of the dots at the peaks and less pressure to make smaller dots as you move to the sides.

Pipe the larger dots around the door, leaving room for a small dot in between.

Pipe dots for the two flowers on either side of the door and one flower over the window on each side panel. Attach a dragée or pipe a center on each (Fig. 8).

Thin a coffee cup full of icing just a bit. If necessary, strain the icing as described in The Fine Print of Fine Piping. Put a No. 1 or No. 0 tip on your decorating bag and fill it only one third full. Pipe a few teardrops to test the consistency. The icing should flow easily from the tube and maintain its teardrop shape without flattening completely.

Pipe the windowpane cross-hatching and outline the windows.

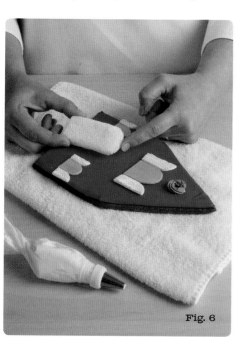

Fig. 6

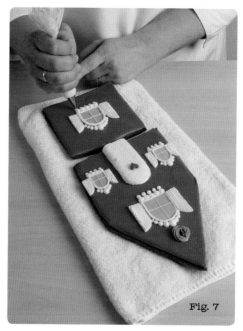

Fig. 7

Fig. 8

Fig. 9

Fig. 10

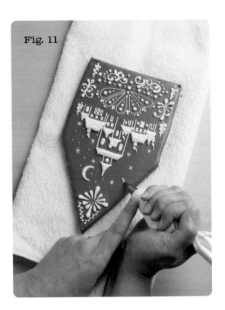

Fig. 11

Pipe the smaller dots.

Pipe the running vines on the front and side panels. Each leaf is a teardrop shape piped at a slight angle. Pipe larger teardrops to create the leaves coming out from each flower.

Pipe large teardrops to look like daisy petals or the rays of a star at the peak of the front panel.

Put the three walls aside to dry, preferably with a fan on them.

Decorate the Back

The back of the house is piped with the No. 0 or No. 1 tip, except for the snowballs underneath the town. Put a clean cloth under the back panel so it will spin easily. I like to start piping in the middle and then work out to the sides. I can turn the cookie to work on it from any angle and generally work without putting my wrist in what I've already done.

Pipe the buildings (Fig. 9). Pipe a thin line underneath them and cover

it with tip No. 10 snowballs using the same medium thick icing you used for the large dots on the front.

Pipe the flower and curlicues underneath the town (Fig. 10).

Turn the cookie upside down and pipe giant teardrops to form the rays of the star. Put a gold dragée in the center. Pipe the moon. Pipe tiny dots and crosses for falling snow (Fig. 11). Pipe the running vines.

Set the back panel aside to dry, preferably near a fan.

Assemble the House

The white piping must be completely dry when you put the house together. Surround the base with plush towels and collect several cans to use as wall supports. Put a towel over each can to protect any white piping it might touch.

Try very hard not to touch any of the white piping! Review the Assembling the House section (page 15). If a wall falls, the white piping

may shatter, and destroy all of your beautiful work.

Position the front panel on the base. Put a can on the wrong side of it (the can will be inside the house) and have a towel-covered can ready if you need to support the front.

Fill a piping bag with thick white royal icing and a large round tip, such as No. 10. Lay a thick line (as thick as your finger) of white icing along the bottom of the front panel and push it firmly onto the base. Put the inside can up against the panel and gently support the front with the towel-covered can. The door should stick out the farthest and it, not your beautiful piping, will most likely touch the can.

Pipe thick lines of white icing on the base where the back and side panels will rest. Attach both sides, then the back following the instruction in Assembling the House on page 15. If the pieces appear unsteady, move the

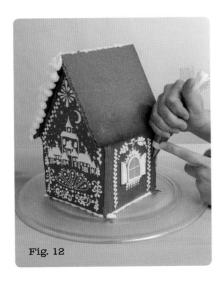
Fig. 12

Fig. 13

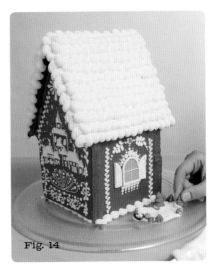
Fig. 14

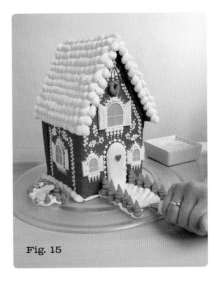
Fig. 15

Fig. 16

towel-covered cans up against them. Press and finesse the four walls together. Remove excess white frosting from the exterior joints with the tip of a butter knife, spatula, or pottery tool.

Use the reserved medium thick red icing and tip No. 47 to pipe red lines over the joints where the walls meet (Fig. 12).

Let the house dry for at least 30 minutes. Attach the roof with the medium thick red icing and let the house dry overnight.

Decorate the Roof

Attach the dry chimney with thick white royal icing. Cover the roof and ends of the roof with rows of downward-facing shells piped with tip No. 20 (Fig. 13). Pipe a small area, then sprinkle coarse sugar for extra shine.

More Decorating

Use a spatula to cover the pond area with a thin layer of white icing. Outline a kidney-shaped pond on top of this with tip No. 10. Set some tiny trees and candy or fondant rocks along the edge (Fig. 14).

Pipe a zigzag front walkway with tip No. 10 and set small green snowman trees on both sides (Fig. 15).

Cover the base with white royal icing and coarse sugar crystals (see Ground Cover, page 88).

Attach white and blue sugar cone trees with white icing.

Tint 2 tablespoons of light corn syrup blue. Use a food-safe paintbrush or small spoon and toothpick to turn the lake a glistening blue. Be careful to not overfill the lake, as the corn syrup will remain liquid (Fig. 16).

MEDIUM KARI'S SKI CABIN

Follow the flow of the directions for the Large Kari's Ski Cabin with the following changes.

- Decrease the Kari's Ski Cabin pattern to 57%.
- Pipe a tiny green wreath with tip No. 14.
- Pipe the snowman trees with tips No. 10 and No. 8. Pipe other trees with open star tips of various sizes.
- Make light blue and white snowflakes using the pastillage recipe on page 10 and the plunger cutter instructions on page 83 (for the snowflake plunger cutters, see Resources, page 131).
- Cover the roof with small white candies (see Tiling a Roof, page 105).
- Pipe tip No. 10 white dots on the edges and ridge of the roof.
- Pipe large zigzags of snow with tip No. 10 or No. 12. Sprinkle on coarse sugar.
- Add the trees, snowflakes, and candies.

SMALL KARI'S SKI CABIN

Follow the flow of the directions for the Large Kari's Ski Cabin with the following changes.

- Decrease the Kari's Ski Cabin pattern to 41%.
- Pipe the snowman trees with tips No. 10 and No. 8. Pipe other trees with open star tips of various sizes.
- Make light blue and white snowflakes using the pastillage recipe on page 10 and the plunger cutter instructions on page 83 (for the snowflake plunger cutters, see Resources, page 131).
- Cover the roof with small white candies (see Tiling a Roof, page 105).
- Pipe tip No. 10 white dots on the edges and ridge of the roof.
- Pipe large zigzags of snow with tip No. 10 or No. 12. Sprinkle on coarse sugar.
- Add the trees, snowflakes, and candies.

Louisa's
Bakery

Snug and inviting, this house welcomes you in. The savory butter cookies, dried nuts, and candied cherries will tempt the appetites of children and adults alike. This gingerbread house exudes charm for all of the winter months, not just during the holidays. To soften and warm the palette, add ivory food coloring to the white icing. To simplify the lighting, use battery operated tea lights as we did in the Haunted Hideaway Halloween house.

TIME-SAVERS

- Leave the windows open and omit the clear sheet gelatin.
- Use battery-operated tea lights that are pushed in through a small door in the back wall instead of the single-socket light kit. The tea lights don't require making a hole in the center of the base (see Interior Lighting, page 96).
- Use battery-operated tea lights surrounding the outside of the house to give it a warm glow.
- Use a much smaller base and surround the house with cookies and chocolates.

- Plaster the roof completely with beautiful cookies and omit the dormer windows.
- Cut the door directly in the front of the house and omit the entryway vestibule.
- Use only white icing to highlight the small cookies and omit the gold luster dust.
- Decorate the house with only store-bought cookies. Use more chocolates for variety.
- Build the fence from pretzels, chocolates, or store-bought cookies.
- Don't light the house at all. Bake solid walls and pipe the windows and door with white icing (Fig. 5).

MAKING THE HOUSE

After you set up the lighting, bake the house, and locate (or make) small cookies, Louisa's Bakery is a snap to decorate.

Light the Base

See Method 2 in the Interior Lighting section (page 97). Test the lights before gluing them onto the base. Take care to keep the cords clear of your work area; yanking on the cord accidentally could pull the entire house down.

The lights below are secured upright by putting hot glue on the metal wings on the light socket element. Don't put hot glue on any plastic components. Make certain the bulbs are upright and won't touch the inside of the house or the base. For a warmer color, put small 7 watt orange or yellow bulbs in the sockets.

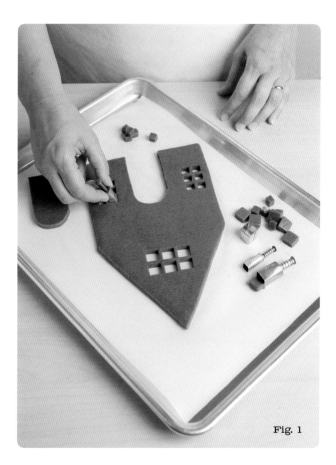

Fig. 1

Fig. 2

Fig. 3

The Pattern

Enlarge the Kari's Ski Cabin pattern, including dormer windows and front vestibule, to 140% and cut out the pattern pieces. The finished house is about 273 mm tall.

Bake the House

Make two recipes of Construction-Grade Gingerbread dough (page 9). Roll the dough ⅜ inch thick on parchment paper.

Cut two house front/back pieces, two sides, and two roof panels.

Cut two mudroom front/back pieces, two mudroom sides, and two mudroom roof panels.

Cut two dormer window fronts, two left sides, two right sides, two left roof panels and two right roof panels.

Freeze the unbaked pieces for 20 minutes to stiffen the dough. Cold dough resists deformation and allows easier and more intricate cuts.

Use a sharp knife to cut a front door in three different cookies—the front panel of the house, and the front and back of the vestibule. All of these must have doors if the interior light is to shine out. Save and bake one door.

Use square plunger cutters to cut windows in the front, back, and side panels and in the dormer window fronts (Fig. 1).

Cut a 1-inch square opening in the very center of each house roof panel. This will allow light to shine through the dormer windows.

Bake at 350°F for about 15–25 minutes, until firm. The smaller pieces will bake more quickly. Let the pieces cool and check them again for firmness. Re-bake if necessary at 275°F until hard. For a shiny surface, glaze the gingerbread following the instructions on page 13.

If you live in a humid area, reinforce the roof panels by covering the wrong side of the cookies with a thin layer of brown royal icing (see Icing the Wrong Side to Increase Strength, page 16). Let them dry.

Fig. 4

Fig. 6

Fig. 5

Bake the Decorations

The cookies for the fence, shutters, and roof and the spritz cookies pictured are homemade. Use small cutters to cut gingerbread cookies in different shapes, bake, and glaze them. Cut the gingerbread fence cookies with a flower-shaped cutter. Cut a circle from the middle with a small round cutter, and use a sharp spatula to slice off the bottom (Fig. 2).

For tiny spritz cookies, use the Spritz Butter Cookies recipe (page 10). Don't refrigerate the dough. Put a large open star tip (I used No. 21) in a disposable plastic decorating bag, add a small amount of cookie

dough, and pipe various shapes onto parchment paper (Fig. 3). If it's too stiff to pipe, warm the dough a bit in your hands. This house has squiggles, stars, rosettes, hearts, and pretzels. To shape the pretzels, pipe a long snake then gently fold it into a pretzel shape. Bake until slightly browned.

Decorate the House

Place the house front, back, and sides and the dormer window fronts wrong side up. Cut pieces of sheet gelatin that are $1/3$–$1/2$ inch larger on all sides than each window opening. Attach a No. 3 tip to a piping bag and add a small

amount of brown royal icing. Outline each window (on the wrong side of the gingerbread) $1/4$ inch from the edge and place the piece of gelatin over the window. Gently press the gelatin down to attach it. Watch that royal icing doesn't squeeze out into the window panel, where it will show. Alternately, simply leave the windows open.

Decorate the front, back, and side panels with small cookies and candies. Decorate the front panel of the vestibule (Fig. 4). Fig. 5 shows piping windows and doors onto an unlit house an a shortcut.

The house pictured has:

- Thick gingerbread shutters with blanched almonds and candied cherries
- Small gingerbread cookies: plain, iced white, covered with jimmies or sprinkles, dusted with coarse sugar, or painted with gold luster dust (see Painting with Luster Dust, page 84)
- Small gingerbread pretzels (make a dough snake, fold it into a pretzel shape, bake, and glaze)
- Small spritz butter cookies
- Small chocolates
- Small, decorative European-style cookies and butter cookies

Build the House, Front Vestibule, and Dormer Windows

Assemble the front vestibule on top of waxed paper using the instructions on page 19 for Assembling the House Separate from the Base. Let it dry. Later you will attach the back wall of the vestibule directly to the front of the house.

Put the front panels of the dormer windows wrong side up and attach the side triangles with brown royal icing (Fig. 6).

Assemble the four walls of the house around the light(s) (see Assembling the House, page 15). Use thick brown icing to join the four walls and white icing to cement the house to the base. Check for adequate clearance around the light bulbs. Allow this to dry for at least 30 minutes.

Use brown royal icing to attach the vestibule to the front of the house.

Use brown royal icing to attach the roof panels and allow the roof to dry at least 30 minutes.

Pipe icing along the bottom edge of the dormer window and up the back of each side triangle. Attach the dormer over the roof's hole on each panel. Allow this to dry at least 30 minutes before you put the small roof panels onto the dormer windows. (See full-page image at left).

More Decorating

Attach small cookies and candies to the roof. Paint gold luster dust on some to add shine (see Painting with Luster Dust, page 84). Use a food-safe paintbrush and thin icing to paint some cookies white.

Outline small heart gingerbread cookies with white royal icing and tip No. 1.

Pipe round dots or zigzags along the house seams to cover messy bits of icing.

Thin a coffee cup full of royal icing just a bit to a medium thin consistency. Pipe round dots along the eaves and drag them down into icicles (see Icicles, page 105).

Pipe upside down teardrops of white icing onto sugar cones to form trees (see Sugar Cone Trees, page 90).

Paint pearl luster dust onto the dry icicles and trees (see Painting with Luster Dust, page 84).

Lay cookies for the front walkway.

To achieve completely smooth snow, cover the base with flood icing (see Flood Icing, page 84). Outline the platter with a large round tip such as No. 12 or snip the end off of a disposable bag to create a larger opening. The barrier outline should rise ¼–½ inch from the base. Thin white icing to flood consistency. Use a decorating bag with a small round tip to flood carefully around the base of the house and any landscaping. Use a larger tip or carefully spoon flood icing to cover open areas of the base.

Sprinkle coarse sugar over the snowy landscape.

Winter Wonderland

This chalet reminds me of snow days spent reveling in the bright winter sunshine. Ready for adventure, a cookie sled lies out back by cinnamon stick woodpiles. A cozy doghouse complete with food, water, and bones shelters Spot. Wander over a bridge cobbled with gingerbread and drop a few candy rocks into the stream below. Or, if warm weather appeals to you, create the same scene for springtime or summer.

TIME-SAVERS

- Put the house on a smaller base. Create only as much landscaping as you wish.
- Create a flat, smooth scene and don't build the hills.
- Omit the bridge, stream, or both.
- Cut a plain gingerbread bridge without adding the cookie cobblestone rocks.
- Ice the doghouse with royal icing and sprinkles instead of tiling it with confetti quins.
- Omit the dog's water and food bowls, or omit the doghouse altogether.
- Construct the front fence with pretzels instead of cutting a gingerbread fence.
- Omit the sled or use a Christmas tree ornament sled if you're certain no one will try to eat it!
- Use holly leaf–shaped sprinkles in the window boxes or pipe green royal icing leaves instead of cutting pastillage holly leaves. You could leave out the window boxes altogether and simply pipe leaves below the windows.
- Cut plain shutters and door without using the wood grain impression mat.

MAKING THE HOUSE

Create the windows first, then the trees and dog bowls so the icing can dry while you bake.

Pattern

Enlarge the Winter Wonderland pattern to 140% and cut out the pattern pieces. The house pictured stands quite tall (about 302 mm tall). You can create an equally dazzling smaller chalet by enlarging the pattern less.

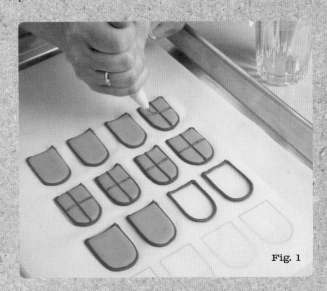

Fig. 1

Make the Royal Icing Transfers

The windows are made using the royal icing transfer method described on page 84. Trace ten windows onto paper (two extras in case some break). Tape this paper down and tape waxed paper over the top. Outline the windows with dark blue medium thick royal icing and a No. 3 tip. Flood the windows with lighter blue flood icing (see Flood Icing, page 84). After the flood icing has crusted, pipe dark blue windowpane crosshatches with tip No. 1 (Fig. 1). Let the windows dry completely before peeling back the waxed paper.

Pipe the Trees

Trees piped as royal icing transfers adorn the chalet's corners. Make three-dimensional trees by joining two royal icing transfers back-to-back or pipe trees on sugar ice cream cones.

HORIZONTALLY PIPED TREES

Pipe different sizes and shapes of trees on a piece of waxed or parchment paper using a No. 18 tip. You need four trees approximately 4 inches tall to cover each of the four house corners and several small landscaping trees.

Pipe four skinny trees about one-half the height of the door. When they're dry, ice them back-to-back to create the two freestanding trees by the front door.

Pipe two large, multilayered trees and add multicolored nonpareils as you pipe. When the trees have dried completely, remove the waxed paper and ice them together back-to-back to create a freestanding Christmas tree.

SUGAR CONE TREES

Pipe five white sugar cone trees of different sizes using a large round tip (see Sugar Cone Trees, page 90). Sprinkle the trees with sugar or edible glitter as you go.

Pipe green sugar cone trees of varying sizes using stars, shells, zigzags, and tall stars (for pine boughs) using tip No. 18.

Pipe two sugar cone trees of lighter green using a large round tip. Make them about two thirds the height of the sugar cone to create the trees where the walkway meets the fence.

Create the Dog Bowls

Cut two small round circles from fondant or pastillage. Use your fingers to coax the edges up to form the sides of a bowl. Let these dry, then apply silver luster dust (see Painting with Luster Dust, page 84). Fill one bowl with brown sprinkles for food and the other with blue icing for water (Fig. 2). If you're building the stream, wait and fill the water bowl with stream water. Add a few dog bone sprinkles.

Fig. 2

Create Pastillage Holly Leaves

Color ½ cup of pastillage green. Cut and emboss (see Using Plunger Cutters, page 83) approximately forty holly leaves and set them aside to dry. Holly-shaped sprinkles or piped green leaves also make wonderful holly.

Bake the House

Make three recipes of Construction-Grade Gingerbread (page 9). Roll the dough ¼–⅜ inch thick on parchment paper. Cut out two house front/back pieces, two sides, and two roof panels. Remove the extra dough and trim the parchment around each cookie. Transfer the parchment-backed cookies to cool baking sheets and bake at 350°F for 15–25 minutes, until firm.

Fig. 3

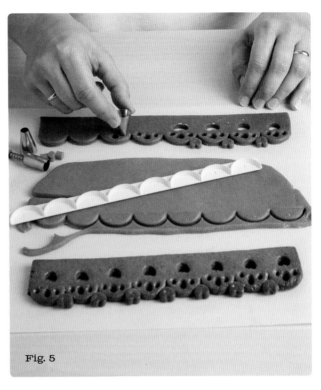

Fig. 5

Fig. 4

Bake the Other Gingerbread Items

Cut eight square closed shutters. Use a knife to cut four vertical lines in each. Cut thin strips of thinly rolled gingerbread to use as the crosspieces.

Paint water in two diagonal lines from corner to corner of each square shutter. Lay one strip of gingerbread diagonally across the shutter from corner to corner. Lay two shorter strips of gingerbread from the other two corners in to meet at the middle. Trim around the entire shutter to remove the overhanging gingerbread (Fig. 3).

Using a wood grain impression mat, cut eight left shutters, eight right shutters, the door, eight window boxes, and the sled top.

Use a nontoxic graphite pencil to trace the pattern for the sled runners onto parchment paper. Roll two gingerbread snakes the diameter of a pencil and lay them onto the patterns.

Cut out a front, a back, and two sides for the doghouse. Cut and remove a door.

Cut the bottom of the bridge and two sides. Make a wad of foil on which to bake the bridge and set it on parchment paper. Cover the mound with a smooth piece of foil, give the foil a spritz of cooking spray, and drape the bridge bottom over it. Put the two bridge sides on parchment and cover each with various tiny balls of gingerbread dough (Fig. 4).

Cut the fence using the pattern on page 117 or the FMM Straight Frill Cutter Set number 9–12 (see Resources, page 131). Cut hearts with a Kemper cutter. Remove each and press it gently into the grooves on top of the fence. Use round tips No. 8 and No. 4 to cut the small circles (Fig. 5).

Bake at 350°F for 8–25 minutes. Watch closely as they bake and remove them before they brown too much. Cover each with a glaze (see Glazing, page 13) and re-bake for 2–5 minutes or until the glaze is set.

Cover the Base

If you recreate this large scene, use a 24 inch by 24 inch piece of plywood as the base. The hills are made from rice cereal treats. Either mold the semi-cool treats into mounds or cut, stack, and carve them (Fig. 6) (see Hills & Valleys, page 95).

Use a large round tip such as No. 12 to pipe both banks of the stream. Pipe across the ends of the stream, too, where it enters and exits the base. Totally enclose the area that will be filled with candy water. Cover the hills with a layer of white royal icing.

Decorate the House

Outline the first floor on each of the four walls then fill the outline with white flood icing. Allow the flood icing to dry completely before attaching the closed shutters and door.

When the white flood icing is dry to the touch, pipe a brown line to separate the first and second floors with tip No. 47 (Fig. 7).

Attach the closed shutters and door with white icing. Surround the door with white dots or small white candies.

Use brown icing to attach the windows, window boxes, and shutters (Fig. 8). Attach the holly leaves with green icing and pipe tiny red berries.

Pipe green garland swags first

Fig. 6

Fig. 7

Fig. 8

Fig. 9

Fig. 10

Fig. 11

Fig. 12

with tip No. 15 and light green icing, then pipe over the garlands again with darker green icing (Fig. 9). Add red royal icing berries with tip No. 1.

Pipe a green wreath with red berries over the door of the doghouse.

Pipe large and then progressively smaller dots along the brown icing border that separates the first and second stories of the house (Fig. 10).

Decorate around the windows. Pipe larger round dots using medium thick royal icing and tips No. 8 and No. 3 (Fig. 11). Pipe smaller dots with slightly thinner royal icing and tip No. 1. Pipe dots around the doghouse door and use a No. 1 tip to pipe the dog's name.

Pipe the scroll work on the front and side panels using medium thin royal icing and a small round tip

such as No. 1 (Fig. 12).

Use a nontoxic graphite pencil to trace the outline of the fireplace on the back panel. Outline the area with white icing using a small round tip. Switch to a large round tip. Cover a 2 × 2 inch section of the fireplace with white icing and press in jellybeans. Work section by section until the fireplace is completed.

Pipe the scrollwork using a No. 1

or No. 0 tip and medium thin royal icing (see The Fine Print of Fine Piping, page 33).

Assemble the House, Doghouse, Bridge, and Sled

Review the Assembling the House section (page 15). Use thick royal icing to join the four walls together. Where white icing meets white icing, pipe white, and where gingerbread meets gingerbread, pipe brown icing. White icing will cement the first story and brown icing will begin with the second story.

Let the house dry for at least 30 minutes. Attach the roof with the brown icing and let it dry overnight. Assemble the dog house with brown icing.

Assemble the bridge and sled with brown icing. Use crumpled foil or cans to support the pieces as they dry (Fig. 13).

Decorate the Roof

Tile the roof with wafer candies. Score and then break the wafers to create half wafers if you want to stagger the tiles as shown (see Tiling a Roof, page 105). Decide where you want the chimney top, attach a gumdrop, and cover it with jellybeans. Use a round tip to pipe a bit of smoke.

Tile the roof of the doghouse with confetti sprinkles—or save an hour and decorate it with anything else.

Add icicles with a No. 5 tip and medium thin icing. If it's too thick, the icing won't pull down into a sharp point; too thin and the icicle will drip down off of the eaves. Pipe a dot and finish it by piping straight down and easing off the pressure. Stop squeezing and pull the icicle into a sharp point.

Other Decorating

Cover the entire board with a thin base coat of white royal icing. Smooth the rice cereal treat hills

Fig. 13

by spreading icing over gaps and ridges. Ease the transition from the board to the riverbank by smoothing icing in the void.

Cover the areas where the house walls join with tip No. 8 zigzags. Use white icing where the first floor white stucco areas meet and brown icing where gingerbread joins gingerbread on the second floor. Attach a piped tree to each corner.

Encircle the house with green gumdrops.

Pipe two white lines to mark both sides of the front walkway. Ice small areas with a spatula or round tip and press in broken candy wafers.

Join two smaller piped trees back-to-back (twice) to form the trees by the front door and attach them with white icing.

Ice a row of spearmint leaves on either side of the walkway then add another row of green gumdrops.

Attach the two lighter green sugar cone trees at the end of the walkway.

Use thick white royal icing and green gumdrops to attach and support the two sections of fence.

Stack foil-covered chocolate drops, large white mint candies, and blue foil-covered chocolate balls to create the two reflecting balls by the front fence.

Spread another layer of thinned white royal icing over base. The icing should be loose enough that sharp peaks sag and lose definition.

Attach the sugar cone pine trees with white icing.

Join the two sprinkle-coated Christmas tree halves back-to-back with green icing. Use white icing to attach them to the base.

Attach the dog house and sled. Join cinnamon sticks with brown icing to form woodpiles.

Shake powdered sugar through a sieve over the scene to create snowfall.

Sprinkle crystilized sugar over the base to create sparkling snow.

Fill the stream and dog's bowl with blue tinted piping gel or corn syrup.

Sweet Retreat

A gingerbread house in red, pink, and white makes a lovely Valentine's Day gift or centerpiece. The grand oak tree in the back sports red candy hearts and carved initials. Lovebirds rest in the spearmint shrubs. To add more color, use large conversation hearts for the fence or to tile the roof. You can lay additional rows of candy along the inside and outside of the fence for more bling.

TIME-SAVERS

- Substitute other candies for the fondant candy canes.
- If you live in an arid environment, use real candy canes (humid air dissolves hard candy into dripping puddles).
- Embellish the door and eaves with small candies instead of white dot patterns.
- Make the tree using green candy for branches or simply pipe a mass of leaves.
- Decorate the back of the house with Valentine's Day candy instead of making the tree.

MAKING THE HOUSE

Make the fondant candy canes and birds first so they can dry. If you prefer a paler or darker shade of gingerbread, see the dough color variations on page 9.

Pattern

Enlarge the Sweet Retreat pattern to 140%. The house is about 223 mm tall. Cut out the pattern pieces for the four walls, large and small round windows, and door.

Create the Fondant Candy Canes and Birds

Use fondant for creating candy canes; pastillage dries too quickly. Use several snakes of pink, red, and white fondant and follow the directions in Making Fondant Candy Canes (page 82).

Make two canes that curl in opposite directions to go by the front door and two small canes that curl in opposite directions to form the heart above the door. Make four straight canes to adorn the four corners of the house. Cut the canes to the proper length.

Use a silicone mold to create white fondant birds (see Molding Fondant or Pastillage, page 81).

Bake the House

Make two recipes of Construction-Grade Gingerbread (page 9). Roll the dough ⅜ inch thick on parchment paper. Cut two house front/back pieces, two sides, and two roof panels. Don't cut out windows or a door from the house walls; leave them solid. Remove extra dough and trim the parchment around each cookie. Cut a door, two large round windows, and one small round window from gingerbread dough. Transfer the parchment-backed cookies to cool baking sheets and bake at 350°F for about 15–25 minutes, until firm.

Ice the Door and Windows

Attach the door to a piece of waxed paper with a dot of icing. Use tip No. 48 and medium thick pink icing to pipe vertical lines on the door. Start each line at the bottom of the door and pipe straight up and over the curved top of the door (Fig. 1). Pipe another line against the first and so on until the door is covered. Immediately add coarse sugar, edible glitter, or luster dust for more shine. Use a knife to trim the extra icing around the top arch of the door (Fig. 2). Let it dry, then snap any extra bits away.

Use a large round tip to pipe pink royal icing on the three round windows. Press each into white or pink sugar and set aside to dry.

Decorate the Back of the House

This grand old oak tree, with its large canopy of branches and carved lovers' initials, adds a touch of nostalgia and romance.

Fig. 1

Fig. 2

Fig. 3

MAKE THE CARVED INITIALS

Color a walnut-sized piece of fondant or pastillage light brown. Press it flat into a thick 1½ diameter circle. Use a toothpick to press initials into the fondant. The initials should be very small; the entire heart shape must fit within the width of the tree trunk.

Mark a heart shape around the initials with a toothpick and trim the excess fondant away with a knife.

MAKE THE TREE LEAVES

If green nonpareils are unavailable, color white nonpareils several shades of green with paste or gel food coloring (see Tinting Nonpareils, Sanding Sugar, and Coconut, page 84). See the Resources section (page 131) for retailers that sell bulk nonpareils. Alternately, you could tint sugar green. Place the sprinkles or sugar in a shallow dish.

Color 1 cup of royal icing green to match the color of your nonpareils.

Lightly mark the outline of your tree trunk and leafy top on the back of the house with a nontoxic graphite pencil. Use a large open star tip such as No. 18 to pipe several balls of icing randomly placed in the leaf area.

Pick up the cookie and gently press the icing balls down into the plated sprinkles. Press only enough to coat the icing, not enough to flatten it. Set the cookie down again and pipe several more balls, press into the

sprinkles and repeat until you have covered the leafy area (Fig. 3).

Use a small round tip and green icing to attach candy hearts, red sugar pearls (apples), or other decoration to the tree.

PIPE ROYAL ICING TRANSFER TREES

While you have the green icing bagged, pipe two or more small green zigzag trees on waxed paper using tip No. 14 and leave them to dry.

PIPE THE TRUNK

Color ¾ cup of royal icing dark brown. To create a streaked effect, stop mixing just before the food coloring is evenly distributed. Bag the icing with an open star tip or tip No. 362.

Start piping at the bottom of the tree; work up and out. Start with the roots. Pipe random lines of roots and build them up in

layers. Pipe one layer of the entire trunk with a set of long lines from the roots up to the leaves (Fig. 4).

Lay the fondant heart with the initials onto the trunk. Pipe more long lines until you're satisfied with the shape and bulk of the trunk. Pipe a heart-shaped outline around the initials (Fig. 5).

Decorate the Front and Sides

Attach the door and a small window to the house's front and a large window to each side.

Attach two fondant candy canes on either side of the door with white icing. Outline the top of the door with pink conversation hearts. Use tiny dots of white icing to add heart-shaped sprinkles on top of these. Accent the door with large icing dots from a No. 10 tip and silver dragées. Add smaller icing dots with No. 5 and No. 1 tips.

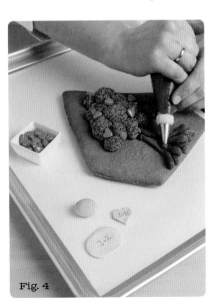

Fig. 4

Fig. 5

Attach two fondant candy canes facing toward each other to form the heart over the door. Pipe white icing inside the heart and cover it with sanding or coarse sugar crystals. Pipe dots with round tips No. 5 and No. 1 surrounding the heart.

Use white or brown icing to attach pink coversation heart shutters on the front and side windows.

Embellish the windows with large and then smaller white dots. Pipe crosshatches with tip No. 1 and dots with tip No. 4 on top of the pink sugar windows themselves.

Let the icing decorating the four walls dry.

Assemble the House

Review the Assembling the House section (page 15). Use thick brown royal icing to join the four walls and white or green icing to anchor it to the base.

Let the house dry for at least 30 minutes. Attach the roof with the brown icing and let it dry overnight.

Decorate the Roof

Tile the roof with pink and white marshmallows. The house pictured uses marshmallows from Arcoiris cookies, which are stocked in grocery stores with other Hispanic cookies and treats. Use a knife to scrape the marshmallow top off of the cookie beneath and attach the marshmallow with white icing. If these specific cookies are unavailable, look for pink and white marshmallows in the baking section of many grocery stores. Valentine's Day candy makers also supply pink, red, and white marshmallows covered with colored sugar.

Use a large round tip such as No. 12 to pipe large white dots along the edge of the roof.

Push a silver dragée, confetti sprinkle, or pink sugar pearl into each dot.

Cover the Base

Working in sections, cover the base with green icing and green coconut (see Ground Cover, page 88). Leave a section open to add the front walkway.

While the grass is wet, brush away any excess coconut and begin work on the fence.

Build the Fence before the Grass Dries

The trough for the fence must be marked and scraped before the icing under the grass dries. It is, however, much easier to add the front path and trees first, so if time allows, skip ahead, do the path and trees, then return and complete the fence.

Fig. 6

Fig. 7

The fence begins 2 inches on either side of the front path. Use a sharp knife or pottery tool to scrape a line about ½ inch from the edge of the base that starts and ends 2 inches from either side of the front walkway. You're doing more than marking the fence line; you're scraping a trough in the icing and coconut that will contain and help hold up the fence. Make the trough roughly ¼ inch across (Fig. 6).

Score and break the candy wafers in half. The house pictured uses pink wafers in front with white wafers offset in back to provide support and contrast. Working in small sections, pipe green icing into the fence trough and push in a line of pink half wafers. Add the offset half wafers in back to keep the fence stable (Fig. 7). It doesn't take much icing to keep the half wafers standing after they're supported in back by the second row. Pipe the tip No. 16 green shell border after the house is complete to avoid sticking an accidental finger in it as you finish decorating.

Other Decorating

Pipe white icing onto the pathway area and press in multicolored nonpareils or other sprinkles.

Use a sharp knife to trim fondant candy canes to the correct length and attach them to the four corners of the house with brown icing.

Surround the house with spearmint leaves and green gumdrops. Slice white gumdrops in half and use the bottoms together with pink and green foil–wrapped chocolates to decorate around the green trees.

Add the two small royal icing transfer trees on either side of the door. Line both sides of the walkway with pink gumdrops.

Add foil-covered chocolate hearts.

Birthday Picnic

A gingerbread house is a wonderful centerpiece for a birthday celebration. Choose candy colors that complement the party décor or are favorites of the birthday boy or girl. The large, grassy lawn leaves room for the picnic or other scene of your choice. Scatter brightly colored sprinkles on the grass for a festive look. To add candles, pipe thick green icing at intervals along the gumdrop border and press them in.

TIME-SAVERS

- Instead of creating the tiny cakes, make two cupcakes by swirling royal icing or a snake of pastillage on top of two chocolate caramel cups or peanut butter cups. Score and break real birthday candles to a shorter length and push them into the icing.
- Use spearmint leaves all along the house sides and omit the sugar cone pine trees.
- Instead of balloons, pipe "Happy Birthday [name] and [name]" on that side of the house (do the piping before you assemble the walls).
- Cut the picnic table pieces from plain gingerbread without embossing the wood grain pattern. Replace the picnic table and cakes with mini or full-sized real cupcakes and the correct number of candles.
- Cut store-bought cookies to create the front steps

MAKING THE HOUSE

Pipe the sugar cone trees and cut the pastillage or fondant windows first so they have time to dry.

The Pattern

Enlarge the Birthday Picnic House pattern to 140% and cut out the pattern pieces. The house is about 330 mm tall.

Create the Pastillage Items

Make a double recipe of pastillage, or purchase fondant, and review Fondant and Pastillage (page 80). Set aside one quarter of the pastillage to remain white. Tint one quarter yellow and one quarter blue. Divide the remaining quarter into small balls and tint each the color of a balloon. Cover each ball of pastillage with a very thin layer of white shortening and wrap it tightly in plastic wrap.

MAKE THE WINDOWS, SHUTTERS, DOOR, AND BALLOONS

Cut seven square yellow windows. Use the edge of a spatula or knife to mark the panes (Fig. 1).

Texture the blue pastillage with ridged roller and cut fourteen rectangular shutters. Use a knife to trim the ends to angles.

Cut a rectangular door from the blue pastillage and make a small indentation where the door handle will go.

Use pliers to modify a small round cookie cutter (Fig. 2). Cut a

Fig. 1

Fig. 2

Fig. 3

Fig. 4

Fig. 5

Fig. 6

Fig. 7

Fig. 8

Fig. 9

balloon of each color. Pat down the edges with your fingers to round and smooth them.

MAKE THE BIRTHDAY CAKES

Roll piece of white pastillage 1–1½ inch thick and cut the birthday cakes using a small round cookie cutter. After the cake has dried for 24 hours, take a sharp knife and carve some of the damp pastillage from the bottom so it's lighter and dries faster (Fig. 3).

Color golf ball–sized pieces of pastillage pink and blue. Make ten tiny ribbon roses of each color (Fig. 4) (see Ribbon Roses, page 94).

The tiny candles pictured were made with a garlic press but you can also make them by rolling out tiny snakes of pastillage. Make extra snakes to allow for breakage. Let the snakes dry, then use a sharp knife to score off candle lengths. Snap the excess off and you have candles!

To create the candles with a garlic press, push the remaining pink and then blue pastillage through a garlic press. Hold the press upside down to let the extruded pastillage hang straight down (Fig. 5). Use a knife to cut several strands at a time from the garlic press and lay them down on waxed paper, taking care keep them as straight as possible. Many of the strands will not be straight, so keep on pressing candles until you have enough mostly straight lengths. Let these dry before delicately separating one length from another. Use a sharp knife to score and then snap them into the correct lengths.

Cut a square of waxed paper to go under each cake. Set the paper and cake on top of a spice bottle. Use your smallest star tip No. 13 to pipe lower and upper shell borders (Fig. 6).

Attach the roses with dots of white icing. Pipe tiny green teardrops for leaves (Fig. 7).

Attach the candles with stars of white icing (Fig. 8).

Make the Sugar Cone Trees

Color thick royal icing dark green using the colors Leaf Green and a small bit of Royal Blue. Pipe sugar cone pine trees following the instructions on page 90 (Fig. 9). The house pictured has one tree made with four stacked sugar cones, one tree made from three stacked sugar cones, and two trees made slightly shorter than the height of a single sugar cone.

Bake the House and Picnic Table

Make two recipes of Construction-Grade Gingerbread (page 9). Roll the dough ¼–⅜ inch thick on parchment paper. Cut out two house front/back pieces, two sides, and two roof panels. Remove the extra dough and trim the parchment around each cookie. Transfer the parchment-backed cookies to cool baking sheets and bake at 350°F for about 15–25 minutes until firm.

Use a rock impression mat and round cutters to make the two front steps. Trim the cookies so they will lie flat against the house.

Use a wood grain impression mat to texture the gingerbread used for the picnic table and benches (see

Fig. 10

Fig. 11

Fig. 12

Embossing Gingerbread, page 14).

Glaze (see page 13) the steps, table, and benches after baking.

Decorate the House

Ice the front, back, and two sides using a spatula with a thin layer of white flood icing. Lay the cookies flat and let them dry.

Using a spatula, spread a ¼ inch layer of medium thick white icing evenly across the dried flood icing. Drag an icing decorating comb from one side of the panel to the other to create the look of siding on the house (Fig. 10). The decorating comb isn't long enough to reach completely along the length of the panel, so go back to the side you started on, line up the comb, and comb across the panel again. My comb needed three passes to texture the house's side and two passes for the front or back panel. Let this dry.

Attach the windows, shutters, and balloons with white icing (Fig. 11 and 12). Pipe gray strings on the balloons with tip No. 1. Lay the two front steps against the house to properly position the door

Fig. 13

Fig. 14

Fig. 15

above them. Attach a dragée in the doorknob indentation. Pipe tip No. 8 balls around the windows and door.

Let the four walls dry completely.

Cover the Base

Look at your base and visualize where the house will sit. Working in sections, cover the other areas with green icing and green coconut (see The Base, page 7). While the icing and coconut are still wet, mark the house's position with a toothpick. Scrape off the extra icing and coconut from this area so the house can attach directly to the base (Fig. 13).

Assemble the House

Review the Assembling the House section (page 15). Use thick white royal icing to join the four walls together. Let the house dry for at least 30 minutes, then attach the roof with the white icing and let it dry overnight.

Decorate the Roof

Tile the roof with small cookies (see Tiling a Roof, page 105). Divide sandwich cookies in half and scrape out the filling if you want flatter tiles. Score and then break cookies to create half cookies if you want to stagger the tiles as shown (Fig. 14).

Other Decorating

Cover the areas where the house walls join and along the edges of the roof with tip No. 16 shells.

Ice the underside of the picnic table with a flat layer of brown royal icing to add strength. Push in the table cross legs and use more icing to secure them. Assemble the benches with brown icing.

Let all of these dry before assembly (Fig. 15).

Attach the front steps with green icing.

Attach the sugar cone pine trees with green icing.

Use green icing to attach a row of gumdrops around the base.

Attach spearmint leaf bushes to the sides of the house with white icing.

Pipe a green border outside of the gumdrops with tip No. 20.

Attach the picnic table and benches with green icing. Set the cakes on the table or attach them with brown icing.

Add foil-wrapped chocolate sports balls.

Components

Techniques

What are fondant and pastillage, and how do they behave differently? For many purposes you can use fondant and pastillage interchangeably, and the choice is a matter of personal preference. The projects in this book specify when one is preferred over the other.

FONDANT AND PASTILLAGE

Fondant is a doughlike sugar modeling medium available at many grocery and craft stores. Recipes abound, but it's easiest to buy it premade. Tinting fondant dark enough for strong colors can be challenging, and the color will fade as it dries. Colored commercial fondant has a deeper hue and will maintain it better than fondant colored at home. Fondant contains some fat, such as white vegetable shortening; it will go rancid after a time. Though the surface eventually crusts, fondant remains somewhat soft and pliable. Unused fondant should be kept covered with plastic wrap in the refrigerator.

Pastillage is a sugar-based dough that contains powdered sugar, cornstarch, gelatin, and flavoring. Unlike fondant, pastillage dries rock hard. Conversation heart candies and tinned strong mint candies are made from much the same recipe.

Tinting pastillage into vivid, dark colors is a challenge (just as with fondant), and the color will fade as it dries. Pastillage dries very quickly—unused balls should be covered with a thin layer of white vegetable shortening and wrapped securely in plastic. Store pastillage in the refrigerator. Work quickly and with the minimum amount, because it starts to crust immediately. When dry, pastillage is incredibly robust and strong, although brittle.

Fondant and pastillage both mold, model, and sculpt well. They take on moderate and light colors easily. Knead in small amounts of gel or paste food coloring, keeping in mind that the color will lighten as it dries. Use edible glue (recipe below) to attach pieces to one another. Add cornstarch if the dough is too sticky, and use small amounts of white shortening or drops of water if it's too hard. When using pastillage straight from the refrigerator, giving it a zap in the microwave for only a few seconds can make the dough pliable enough to knead. Use either a dusting of cornstarch or a very thin film of shortening to keep the dough from sticking to your work surface and hands. Dust cutters with cornstarch. It's better to dust the ball of paste than the mold so that only a fine coating of cornstarch is on the surface where it is needed. Cornstarch placed directly into the mold may obscure fine details. If you have trouble releasing the dough, put the mold in the freezer for 10 minutes and try again. To speed up the molding process, sacrifice some detail and dust the mold itself.

Make a Cornstarch Dusting Bag

Fill a square of cheesecloth with a small amount of cornstarch. Tie up the corners and use this bag to lightly dust your hands and work surface (Fig. 1). Molds and impression mats with intricate details or deep cavities should be immersed in cornstarch and then tapped to remove the excess.

Embossing Fondant or Pastillage

Impression mats can create stunning pieces of fondant and pastillage with the texture of cobblestone, brick, wood grain, and many other surfaces. See the Resources section

Fig. 1

(page 131) to locate retailers that carry mats.

Roll the dough a little thicker than your finished piece, because rolling it again under the mat thins it more. Lightly dust the surface of the dough with cornstarch. Dust the mat with cornstarch and tap it to remove the excess. Place the mat on the dough and roll the rolling pin one time only over the length of the mat. Carefully peel the mold away and check to see if the pattern has completely transferred (Fig. 2). If it hasn't, reapply cornstarch to the mold and try again on a new piece of dough. It may take several tries to get a clean impression. Cut out your shape with a cookie cutter or small knife. Use a spatula to lift the piece onto waxed paper to dry.

The wood grain mat I use has deep channels that like to trap pastillage. The trick to removing the mat is bending it up along its length into a taco shape (a long taco rather than a tall taco). This opens up the space between the channels and allows the pastillage to come out.

Molding Fondant or Pastillage

Silicone molds come in many shapes and forms, each a little different and each with its own challenges. Roll a ball of fondant that fits inside the mold's cavity. Dust the ball lightly with cornstarch and press it firmly into the mold. You can also dust the mold with cornstarch and tap it upside down to remove the excess, however cornstarch in the mold can obscure tiny details. Use your thumbs to press the fondant in and to push any excess to the sides. Trim off any extra fondant, then invert the mold and pop it out (Fig. 3). If the fondant sticks, place the mold in the

Fig. 2

Fig. 3

freezer for 10 minutes. Most molds with small details or deep cavities will need to sit in the freezer for 10 minutes before you are able to pop out the fondant.

Marbling Fondant or Pastillage

Sometimes you can achieve a beautiful marbling effect as you mix food coloring into fondant. Take a disk of fondant and streak the food coloring across the top using a toothpick. Fold the fondant in two, twist it a bit, and knead it slowly, watching the colored swirls emerge (Fig. 4). If you knead for too long, the swirls will blend and you have colored fondant.

To marble colored fondant, make a snake of each color. Press and roll them together into a multicolored cane. Twist the bundle and fold it end over end (Fig. 5). Knead it until you reach the desired swirl pattern density (Fig. 6).

When you reroll marbled fondant, the colors will blend and the swirls will disappear.

It's easier to marble fondant than pastillage. The pastillage crusts over so quickly that it must be worked in small amounts, and each bit has to be separately marbled.

Making Fondant Canes

Because standard candy canes melt when exposed to humid air, pastillage candy canes are often used. The

Fig. 4

Fig. 5

Fig. 6

Fig. 7

Sweet Retreat on page 67 has pink, red, and white fondant candy canes. Fondant canes are much easier to create because pastillage canes must be made very quickly.

Color a ball of fondant for each color in your cane. Roll one or two ½-inch diameter snakes of fondant of each color. Do this quickly to keep them moist so they will adhere to each other. Line the snakes up

lengthwise and firmly press them together into one large cane. Start to roll the cane. Try to press the pieces together and elongate the cane with pressure rather than merely rolling and pulling. Too much moisture or too much cornstarch can make rolling difficult. Add finger smears of water or dust the surface lightly with cornstarch, if necessary. Cut the cane in half when it gets too long. When you reach the desired diameter, twist the cane and roll it to create candy stripes (Fig. 7). Cut and mold the lengths to your desired shape.

Measuring Pieces of or Pastillage

There are two quick methods for creating many pieces of the same size. Roll a snake and cut it into segments of equal lengths. Or roll the fondant out and cut perfect circles with a small cutter or the end of a large round piping tip.

Using Plunger Cutters

The snowflakes on Kari's Ski Cabin (page 43) and holly leaves on Winter Wonderland (page 59) are cut with plunger cutters. Dust your surface lightly with cornstarch and roll out fondant or pastillage thin. Dust the cutter with cornstarch and tap it to remove any excess. Hold the cutter and cut the shape. Wiggle the cutter slightly while pressing against your rolling surface to help make a clean cut. Lift the cutter with the fondant inside and run your thumb over the edges to press off any stray bits of fondant.

If your cutter has an embossed pattern as the holly leaves and snowflakes do, place it back on the surface. Press the plunger to emboss the patterns (Fig. 8).

Hold the cutter over waxed paper or foam pad and push the plunger to release the fondant (Fig. 9).

Fig. 8

Fig. 9

PAINTING WITH LUSTER DUST

Luster dust can be applied as a powder directly to fondant, icing, or cookies or can be mixed with vodka or almond extract and painted on. To paint with luster dust, put 4–5 drops of vodka or almond extract in a small container. Add a small amount of the dust and mix to form a paint. The paint should be fluid and shiny with a rich color. If it's too thin, the coverage won't be complete. If it's too thick it won't flow enough to paint with a brush. Use a food-safe paintbrush to paint this onto your item. Some of the roof cookies on Louisa's Bakery (page 53) are painted with gold luster dust.

Several different dust-type products are available. Some of these are safe to eat and some are not. Take note when you purchase your dust and read the label carefully if you intend for the item to be eaten.

TINTING NONPAREILS, SANDING SUGAR, AND COCONUT

White sprinkles, sugar, and coconut can be tinted with a bit of paste or gel food coloring. Put the sprinkles in a plastic bag. Use a toothpick to add a small amount of food coloring and knead the entire bag until the color is smooth and even (Fig. 10). Pour the sprinkles into a bowl and leave them out to dry.

ROYAL ICING TRANSFERS

Pipe royal icing on waxed paper, let it dry, then remove the paper, and you have a royal icing transfer. Transferring dried royal icing opens up many possibilities. You can make decorations ahead of time. If you need four trees you can make six and choose the best ones. You can lay the royal icing pieces on your house panels and move them about

to decide what arrangement looks best. You can discard a mistake instead of meticulously scraping it off of the house.

Many of the decorations in this book, including wreaths, trees, windows, and flowers, were made as royal icing transfers.

Use a few dots of icing to attach a piece of waxed paper to a tray, cookie sheet, or cutting board. If you're making trees, pipe the trees on the paper, plus a test blob of icing, and let everything dry. When you're ready to remove the trees, remove the test blob first. Make certain it's completely dry. There's often less breakage if you remove the paper from the trees instead pulling the trees off the paper. Support and lift each tree with one hand while peeling the paper away with the other.

Windows made with flood icing are great candidates to make ahead of time and transfer. Decorations made with flood icing will be more delicate, so make extras and handle them with care.

FLOOD ICING

To flood with icing is simply to pipe a border and then fill the interior with icing. Flood icing is the consistency of honey or syrup and dries to a shiny, smooth surface.

You can flood a large area such as the entire face of a gingerbread house. Kari's Ski Cabin on page 43 uses this method to create the red walls. This flooding is done directly

Fig. 10

onto the cookie. Smaller areas, such as the windows for the Winter Wonderland House on page 59, can be done on waxed paper, dried, and then transferred to the house.

Color your icing before you thin it and set aside enough to pipe outlines. Thin the icing to a flood consistency by adding small amounts of water. To thin 1 cup of icing, start by adding 1 teaspoon of water, then add water drop by drop. To test it, lift up some icing with a knife and let it drip back into the bowl. You have achieved a good flood consistency when the drip in the bowl disappears into the icing around in about 10 seconds. When you fill your area, flood icing that is too thick will resist settling into a smooth surface. Flood icing that's too thin may jump the barrier and take forever to dry. See Fig.31 on page 23 for a photo demonstrating the correct consistency.

Mark the flood area on a cookie with a nontoxic graphite pencil or lightly scratch it with a corsage pin. If you're using a pattern for a royal icing transfer, tape the paper down and tape waxed paper over the pattern.

Outline the area to form a barrier. Use a No. 3 tip and pipe a line of medium thick royal icing along the limits of the area (Fig. 11). Lay down the line of icing smoothly; breaks or dips in the line allow flood icing to escape. To repair a break or connect the end of the line to the beginning, dip a food-safe paintbrush in water and gently coax the icing bits together.

If you are outlining and flooding with the same color, let the outline dry a few minutes until it crusts over. If the flood icing is a different color, let the outline dry completely to prevent one color bleeding into the other.

Fold back the top cuff of a disposable decorating bag and set it in a heavy glass. Pour the flood icing into the bag, filling it no more than halfway.

If you're filling a small area, snip

Fig. 11

Fig. 12

Fig. 14

Fig. 13

Fig. 15

a small bit off the end of the bag to create a small hole. Large areas fill more quickly with larger openings. The icing will immediately begin to run out of the bag. Setting it back in the glass will stop most drips and contain the rest.

Start filling in the area with flood icing (Fig. 12). Drag the tip of the bag to smooth it around and use a toothpick to coax it into corners. You want the volume of icing to settle flat with the surface only slightly higher than the outline. As the icing settles, any excess will ooze over the barrier, so take care not to overfill. Gently shake the cookie or tap it on the table to help the icing settle and smooth. Pop any air bubbles with a corsage pin or toothpick.

Let the flood icing dry completely if you plan to pipe decorations on top. This is especially important if the icing colors are different. Strongly tinted icing can bleed its color into any other icing it touches. Letting one dry before applying the next minimizes this. Use a fan to speed things up.

Fig. 16

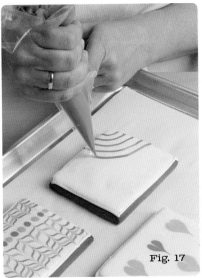

Fig. 17

Fig. 18

USING THE WET-ON-WET ICING TECHNIQUE

Wet-on-wet icing is just what it says—wet (flood) icing applied over wet (flood) icing (Fig. 13–18). The Haunted Hideaway on page 37 has a spiderweb roof done with the wet-on-wet technique. This is an easy, straightforward method to create sophisticated patterns.

Remember that the key to making this method work is that both (or all) icings must still be wet. Prepare first and then work without interruption.

Wet-on-wet areas usually start with flooded areas, so read the section above on working with flood icing. Prepare a decorating bag with a No. 3 tip and medium thick royal icing of your desired color. Prepare

flood icing in the flood color and the accent colors. Load each color into a separate disposable decorating bag. Set each bag upright in a cup or glass and move them right next to your working area.

Outline the area and fill it with flood icing. Snip a small bit off of another bag and pipe lines, dots, or squiggles onto the flood icing. Continue with the other colors.

Because the flood icing and accent icings are the same consistency, the accents will sink down and create a level surface.

Drag a toothpick, corsage pin, or turkey lacer through the accent dots or lines to form patterns.

GROUND COVER

Surround your house with a landscape of glistening white, lush green, or anything in between:

+ Shredded green coconut as grass
+ Shredded white coconut as snow
+ Powdered sugar shaken through a sieve to create snow
+ Green or white icing as grass or snow
+ Green or white sprinkles as grass or snow
+ Crushed graham crackers or brown sugar as sand
+ Crushed chocolate cookies as dirt
+ Blue icing and piping gel as water

Fig. 19

Any morsels or crumbs should be thoroughly embedded in a layer of like-colored royal icing.

After deciding on the ground cover, you have another important choice: add it before you cement the house down (onto the bare base) or after.

There are some advantages to laying ground cover after you anchor the house:

+ The house is very firmly attached to the base. The dry royal icing should keep it in place, even if you tilt and swirl.
+ The house itself is cemented directly onto the base without interference from coconut grass, cookie dirt, etc.
+ Only exposed areas are covered, saving materials.

There are other advantages to laying ground cover on the base beforehand:

+ The base is wide open, making it quick and easy to cover.
+ The house can be made detachable, as with the small Haunted Hideaway on page 37, so it can be lifted up to turn interior lights on and off.
+ You can scrape away the coconut under the house's footprint so that it's cemented directly onto the base.

Royal Icing as Ground Cover

Royal icing makes excellent ground cover. A base covered with royal icing helps anchor and support the house and candy. A large round tip creates puffy clouds of snow or mounds of grass. Decorating tips No. 233 and No. 234 pipe tufts of grass. Use a spatula to spread a smooth layer. Add sparkling sugar, edible glitter, or sprinkles for more color and texture.

Coconut as Ground Cover

Further shred shredded unsweetened coconut in a food processer to make it finer. The smaller the coconut particles, the easier it is to attach items on top with icing. Add food coloring while the coconut is in the food processor for quick coloring or put it in a plastic bag and knead in the coloring.

COCONUT, SPRINKLES, CRUMBS, OR OTHER TASTY MORSELS AS GROUND COVER

The goal is to firmly embed the food particles into royal icing of a matching color.

1. Color the royal icing. The amount of icing will depend on the size of your base and whether you intend to pipe borders or other landscaping with the same color. Match the color of the icing to the color of your ground covering: white for snows, green for grasses, or brown for dirt.

2. Designate a small area and spread a layer of icing just thick enough so that you can't see the base. It needn't look flawless, but should cover all of the area. Holding the base in one hand, immediately press a generous amount of coconut or crumbs onto the icing with the other. Do this over a piece of waxed paper to reclaim what falls off. Press again to force the coconut down into the icing and dust the excess away. The material should be embedded in the icing and not resting on top of it. Excess coconut or crumbs that aren't thoroughly iced down will prevent you from attaching other things.

3. Cover the remaining areas and brush away excess crumbs.

4. Mark the house's footprint with a toothpick and scrape away the icing and crumbs within. When you assemble the house, you'll be able to cement it directly to the base without interference from the grass or snow.

5. Use like-colored royal icing to cement down the house or, if you already have, decorate!

6. If the base dries before adding other objects, you should vigorously brush the excess coconut or crumbs away (Fig. 20). If there is loose coconut or sugar, the objects join with it instead of the base and fall away later.

Fig. 20

WATER

You can create bodies of water, big or small, using several methods. All of the following can represent water:

◆ Blue royal icing
◆ Blue piping gel
◆ Blue-colored light corn syrup
◆ Blue fondant or pastillage
◆ Blue fruit leather
◆ Blue chocolate candy coating
◆ Blue hard candies, crushed and melted
◆ Blue taffy candy, flattened and shaped

Pipe a stream's banks with royal icing and a large open tip. Let your ground cover meet and cover the banks. Outline a pond the same way. Flood it with blue icing for a smooth surface. Paint piping gel or a thin layer of corn syrup on dried icing to give it a shine. Roll out blue taffy-type candies to make ponds. Blue fruit leather can be cut to shape. Blue candy coating can be melted and shaped like a pond. If you live in an arid environment, crush and melt blue hard candies (Fig. 21).

TREES

Trees piped with green icing add color and charm to any house. If you prefer, use green spearmint leaves, gumdrops, gumballs, or sprigs of rosemary.

Sugar Cone Trees

Sugar cones meant for ice cream provide an excellent base for pine trees of all sizes. Cover the cones with sprinkles, coconut, coarse sugar, dried parsley flakes, or piped green icing. For taller trees, stack sugar cones with a bit of icing to connect them. Decorate the entire stack as one tree. For shorter trees, start partway up the cone and continue to the top. After the icing has dried, break off the uncovered cone.

To cover the trees with coarse sugar, coconut, or sprinkles, use a spatula to spread like-colored icing on the sugar cone, roll it in the topping, and allow it to dry.

PIPING ICING ON SUGAR CONE TREES

There are many ways to pipe icing and form sugar cone trees. I find it easier to work with the cones if I hold them upside down with the point in my left hand. Start piping at the large end of the cone and work down to the point. Try to stagger the individual leaves or branches to make them appear more random. As you come close to finishing the tree, your handhold will get smaller and smaller until you need to right the cone. Turn it right side up and set it on waxed paper to pipe the top point.

Fig. 21

Fig. 22

Use medium thick royal icing to prevent the icing from drooping or sliding down the cone. Thicker icing will tire your hand more, so only load the decorating bag one third full to ease the strain. You can also beat some more air into the icing to make it less dense. Fluffier icing is easier to pipe yet still stiff enough.

Royal icing crusts quickly enough that sprinkles must be added in sections as you pipe. Pipe a little, add sprinkles, pipe some more, and add more sprinkles.

STAR TREE

Use an open star tip to pipe stars over the entire surface of the cone. Keep the individual stars close together and staggered.

TEARDROP TREE

Use large open star or round tip to make teardrop- or shell-shaped branches. Hold the cone upside down and pipe a row of shells along the bottom edge. Continue down the length of the cone, taking care to stagger the branches. Set the cone upright on waxed paper to pipe shells on the tip.

LEAF TREE

Use tip No. 349 or No. 352 to create leaves. Hold the cone upright by its point, encircle the cone's lower edge with downward-pointing leaves. Continue working your way up the cone.

PINE TREE

Use a large open star tip such as No. 20 to pipe pine tree branches. Use thick royal icing to keep branches pointed up. Each branch is a modified star. Touch the tip to the cone and squeeze. Build the star up to a tapered point, stop squeezing, and pull away. You want to create a star shaped like a tall building instead of a flat star with a curly tail. Angle the decorating bag at 45° to the cone and pipe each branch slightly upward (Fig. 22).

ZIGZAG TREE

Use a large open star or round tip to pipe zigzags around the cone. Hold it upside down, pipe a running zigzag around the bottom edge, and continue to pipe overlapping layers of zigzags until you reach the top.

COIL TREE

Use a very large star tip and lay ropes of icing in a coil around the cone.

Rice Cereal Treat Trees

Make a recipe of rice cereal treats and add green food coloring to the melted marshmallows before adding the cereal. Mold or cut the green treats into trees. If you used uncolored treats cover them with royal icing or use the icing to glue on colored coconut or sprinkles.

Fondant Trees

Mold green fondant into a cone. Leave the surface smooth, or texture it by scoring it repeatedly with an open star tip.

Roll a long green fondant snake with one end larger and the other end tapered. Starting with the larger end, roll the snake into a vertical coil, making each successive layer smaller. The tapered end will stick up to form the treetop.

Piping Trees as Royal Icing Transfers

Royal icing transfers are a snap to make, and you can store them for months in a cool, dry place. If you plan to decorate the trees with sprinkles, attach your paper to a pan with edges so you can reclaim the runaway candies.

TREES PIPED HORIZONTALLY

Tape down a piece of waxed paper on your work surface or on a tray, cookie sheet, or flat cutting board. Read the Royal Icing Transfers section (page 84). Use stars, dots, teardrops, or zigzags to pipe trees on the paper.

When dry, remove the paper and stand the trees up alone or use icing to join them back-to-back to create a more three-dimensional tree.

Some Ideas for Piping Trees

◆ Pipe zigzags of medium thick green royal icing in a tree shape with an open star tip or round tip. Use larger tips for larger trees. To make these stand out more, pipe a second, smaller tree on top of the first. Add sprinkles immediately.

◆ Pipe with a circular motion to create ropelike trees. The circular piping motion stacks the icing up like the curled cord of an old telephone or a spring.

◆ Pipe stars in the shape of a tree. Make certain they're closely spaced and consider piping more than one layer to make the tree more sturdy.

◆ Pipe teardrops with a large round tip or shells with an open star tip and stack them closely. Overlap each row on top of the previous row.

TIP: Attach two trees with royal icing back-to-back to create a standing three-dimensional tree.

Fig. 23

Fig. 24

THREE-DIMENSIONAL TREES PIPED VERTICALLY

Snowman trees are piped with a round tip. Pipe the bottom and largest layer first—a giant ball. Keep squeezing and let the ball build around your tip. Stop squeezing, lift the tip up a fraction of an inch, and pipe another slightly smaller ball on top. Keep adding layers and decreasing their sizes until you can pull the top of the tree into a nice peak. Pipe spheres and not pancakes, because the weight of each successive layer will flatten the layers beneath. If they start out round,

they'll keep a better shape. For trees taller than 2 inches it's helpful to make the lowest, biggest level and let it sit for a few minutes before piping the next largest ball on top of it, and so on until the tree is finished (Fig. 24).

Pipe Swirling Trees using an open star tip such as No. 21. Pipe green medium thick icing around a large gumdrop. Smaller open star tips can swirl icing around small gumdrops. For even smaller items, pipe tall swirls without the gumdrop. A tall star forms tiny trees. Immediately add sprinkles or dragées for decoration.

TOPIARIES

Coat gumballs or dried balls of pastillage with like-colored medium thick royal icing and tinted coconut or dried parsley flakes. For a color variation, work a small amount of toasted coconut or some graham cracker crumbs into green coconut. You can also pipe small trees with green medium thick royal icing and attach these to flowerpots to form topiaries. Small caramel-filled chocolate cups or peanut butter cups make easy flowerpots, or model pots from pastillage (see Flowerpots, page 94).

HEDGES

Cut rice cereal treats into long rectangles and join them together to form hedges. Cover with green icing and coat with green coconut or dried parsley flakes.

HOLLY LEAVES

Purchase holly leaf sprinkles and attach them with dark green icing, pipe dark green icing leaves to represent holly, or use a holly leaf plunger cutter (see Resources, page 131) to cut pastillage holly leaves. Use red sprinkles, red candy pearls, or dots of red icing for berries.

FLOWERS

Flowers in pots, on shrubs or trees, or even peeking from under the snow add charm to any gingerbread house.

Ribbon Roses

Molding ribbon roses from fondant or pastillage is a breeze. Roll out a snake of fondant and slightly flatten it. Starting at the narrowest end, roll the fondant up as you would a sleeping bag (Fig. 25). Pinch the bottom of the rose to narrow it and help flare out the petals.

Dot-Swirl Flowers

Dot-swirl flowers are made as royal icing transfers by piping flat dots of medium thick royal icing onto waxed paper. Let these dry, then pipe a swirl on top using a smaller round tip. Make the swirl a slightly darker or lighter shade of icing for more contrast.

Plunger Cutter Flowers

Use pastillage or fondant with daisy plunger cutters. Pipe an icing center, or use icing to attach sprinkles.

Flower-shaped Kemper cutters make small scalloped flowers from fondant or pastillage. Push the center in a bit with a rounded tool to push up the petals.

Other Flowers

✦ Use flower-shaped sprinkles or small flower-shaped candies.

✦ Pipe rosettes on waxed paper with royal icing and let them dry.

✦ Pipe small dots of icing for tiny flowers.

Fig. 25

FLOWERPOTS

Upside-down gumdrops, chocolate caramel cups, and small peanut butter cups all make excellent flowerpots.

You can also mold flowerpots from pastillage. Use Terra Cotta food coloring, or mix red and brown together to get the right color. Put a small ball of the pastillage on the end of a chopstick. Roll the ball and chopstick back and forth on your work surface to flatten the sides and form a pot shape. Use a sharp knife to trim off the uneven top as you roll. Gently remove the pot and allow it to dry (Fig. 26).

ROCKS

Nothing suits the fancy of a child more than eating sugar rocks! Finally the universe has created and delivered a rock meant to put in your mouth. It's pure magic! You know the child at the birthday party who asks for one of the big roses

Fig. 26

Fig. 27

on his piece of cake? He wants the rocks, too.

Use chocolate or jellybean-type candy rocks or model rocks out of fondant. Pastillage rocks work just as well, but they dry rock hard, so I prefer fondant because it's kinder to the teeth.

See the Marbling Fondant or Pastillage section (page 82). Use cornstarch on your work surface and hands if the fondant is sticky. Tint fondant into different ivories, browns, grays, and dark grays.

While you knead food coloring into the fondant it may naturally become marbled as the color streaks through. If so, stop kneading and make rocks. If not, roll small snakes of each color, wind them together, fold them over, and knead just until you reach a marbled state. Form rocks of different sizes and shapes and set them aside on waxed paper to dry.

HILLS & VALLEYS

Sculpt smaller hills and valleys with thick, fluffy royal icing and a spatula. Cover stacked graham crackers or small mounds of rice cereal treats with icing. Use a spatula to smooth the transition between elevations.

Larger hills require rice cereal treats molded into a hill shape or stacked and carved into a hill shape. Winter Wonderland (page 59) has two hills modeled with rice cereal treats. Cover the treats completely with royal icing.

Lighting

Lights throw an irresistible glow onto a gingerbread house. Even the quickest lighting plan—tea lights around the base of a house—warms the scene and draws you in.

INTERIOR LIGHTING

Battery-operated tea lights, battery-operated mini light strings, and single-socket light kits all add a lovely glow coming from the open windows and door of a gingerbread house. Single-socket light kits are available at craft stores and take a small 7 watt nightlight bulb.

Never use the open flame of a candle.

Take care with lights because they are inedible! If tiny hands or paws decide to eat from the house, they could try to eat the lights. If you have children or dogs, use removable lights and don't leave the lighted house unattended.

To light a house from within, you need open spaces for the light to shine out, a light source, and a way to turn the light off and on. I use three different methods to add light to the inside of gingerbread houses.

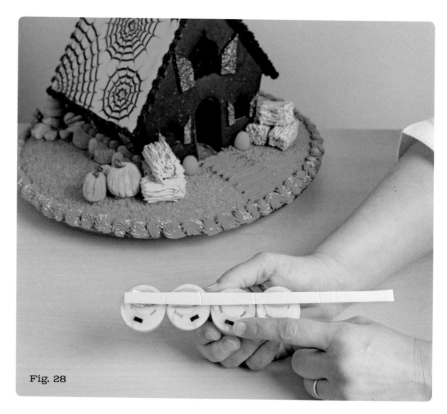

Fig. 28

Fig. 29

Fig. 30

Bundle and secure them with a rubber band, leaving the cord and plug hanging free. Decorate the house. Assemble the front and two side walls. Lay the bundle of lights inside the house and lead the cord under the notch as you attach the back wall (Fig. 30). Check the cord's length and plug it in to test the lights again. Take care to keep the bulbs themselves away from the wall. Use royal icing, or masking tape followed by royal icing, to secure the wires in place. Now add the roof.

Method 2:
Build the Lights into the Base

Two modifications to the base are necessary to build the light itself into the house. First, your base must have a hole in the center of it. Plywood or multiple layers of corrugated cardboard work well. Second, the base must be raised to allow the electrical cord space to go under the base and up through the central hole. Hot glue two strips of wood parallel to each other on either side of the base to lift it up a centimeter or so. Four paint stirring sticks (Fig. 32) stacked two and two works well. New pencils will also give you adequate clearance. Rig a single-socket 7 watt light to enter up through the hole in the base. Use modeling clay or hot glue on the metal wings to keep it standing upright (Fig. 33). The cord will exit the bottom of the base and continue

Method 1:
Cut an Access Port in the Back of the House

This is by far the easiest way to light a house. Before baking the back of the house, cut a small door at the bottom middle of the back cookie. Make the door large enough for tea lights to pass through. Allow some extra clearance in case the dough spreads.

Decorate and assemble the house and leave a path clear from the edge of the base to the access port. Use hot glue to attach tea lights to a strip of corrugated cardboard. Align the lights so the switch on the bottom of each hangs over the side of the cardboard (Fig. 28). To light the house, turn the tea lights on and push them inside with the cardboard strip (Fig. 29).

Rig a string of lights inside the house with a one-inch access notch. Cut the notch along the bottom of the back panel before baking.

TIP: Check the lights to make certain they work!

Fig. 31

Fig. 32

Fig. 33

through the void underneath provided by the wooden strips. Consider rigging two lights through the base, in case one bulb burns out. Turning the lights on is as easy as flipping the switch.

Method 3: Lift the House!

This works only with small, robust gingerbread houses. The house interior must be large enough to hold a tea light. Decorate your house as usual, but assemble the four walls on top of waxed paper instead of on the base. Reinforce the inside of the corners with extra icing before adding the roof panels. When the icing is dry, lift the house and peel back the waxed paper. Put the house on the base and decorate around it without adding candy or icing that touches. After all has dried, lift the house up and down to turn the tea light on and off.

EXTERIOR LIGHTING

Battery-operated tea lights, mini light sets, and traditional light strings add warmth and depth to the scene. All are inedible, of course. If you have the house around children or pets, drape or set the lights on the house and base after everything is dry. Remove the lights whenever the house is unattended.

WINDOWS

DOORS

FIREPLACES

ROOFS

TILING A ROOF

Candy wafers, small cookies, sticks of gum, chocolate disks . . . there are so many choices for roof tiles. Here are some things to consider when you choose your tiles and put them on.

✦ The lighter the tiles, the better. Thick, heavy candies can look awkward and may collapse the roof.

✦ The smaller the tiles, the more in scale your house will appear. Tiny tiles applied in straight rows are stunning.

✦ The smaller the tiles, the more time it will take to put them on. Consider how much time you want to spend roofing.

✦ Tiles can be set in a line or staggered. See the photo at left for examples of each. Staggered tiles are offset by one half of their width, so you may need to score and snap tiles in half to complete every other row.

✦ Tile the roof *after* the house is assembled. If the roof panel is slightly askew, you will want to line up the tiles with the level base and not the edge of the roof. Also, some types of candies or cookies extend below the edge of the roof and cover up the area where the roof and side meet.

Check your roof. Is it level with the base? Pipe a straight line that is level with the base across the roof and use the line for guidance.

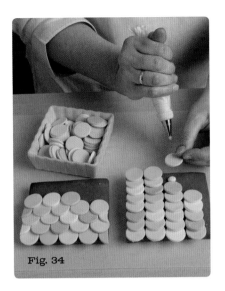

Fig. 34

Fig. 35

Pipe white icing along the bottom edge. Always work from bottom to top. One by one, firmly push tiles into the icing until you reach the other side. Adjust the line of tiles up or down and right or left to center it on the roof and align it with the base. You may need to use a half tile to finish off the row.

If you stagger the tiles, begin the next row with a half tile. Lay the tiles so they overlap the previous row. If you want to keep the tiles inline start the next row exactly as you did the first (Fig. 34).

COVERING THE EDGE OF A ROOF

Covering the edge of a roof gives it a tidy, finished appearance. Icicles have a cool, wintery look while piped trim can be used in any season and allows you to embellish with small candies.

Icicles

Pipe icicles with a small round tip and medium thin icing. If it's too thick, the icing won't pull down into a sharp point; too thin and the icicle itself will drip down off of the eaves. Pipe a dot and finish it by piping straight down and easing off the pressure. Stop squeezing and pull the tail to a sharp end (Fig. 35).

Piped Trim

Use medium thick icing and an open star tip or round tip to pipe zigzags, shells, or other patterns.

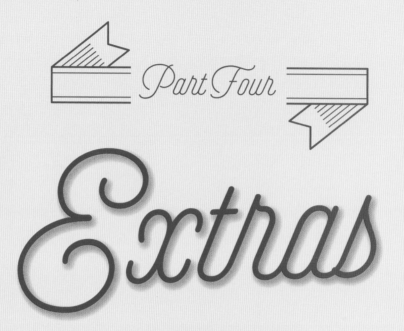

Part Four

Extras

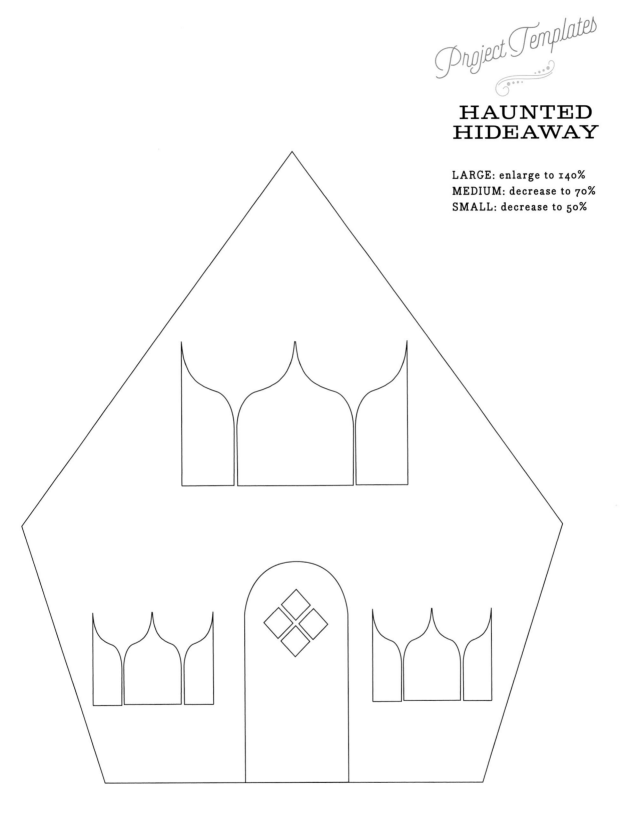

HAUNTED HIDEAWAY

LARGE: enlarge to 140%
MEDIUM: decrease to 70%
SMALL: decrease to 50%

FRONT & BACK

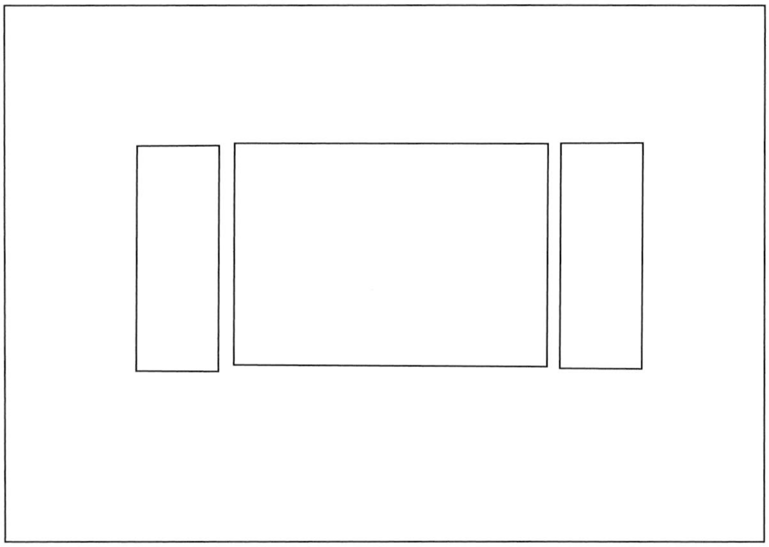

SIDE

LARGE: enlarge to 140%
MEDIUM: decrease to 70%
SMALL: decrease to 50%

ROOF

LARGE: enlarge to 140%
MEDIUM: decrease to 70%
SMALL: decrease to 50%

KARI'S
SKI CABIN

LARGE: enlarge to 140%
MEDIUM: decrease to 57%
SMALL: decrease to 41%

BACK

SIDE
LARGE: enlarge to 140%
MEDIUM: decrease to 57%
SMALL: decrease to 41%

ROOF
LARGE: enlarge to 140%
MEDIUM: decrease to 57%
SMALL: decrease to 41%

FRONT

LARGE: enlarge to 140%
MEDIUM: decrease to 57%
SMALL: decrease to 41%

LOUISA'S BAKERY

BACK

Enlarge to 140%

SIDE

Enlarge to 140%

ROOF

Enlarge to 140%

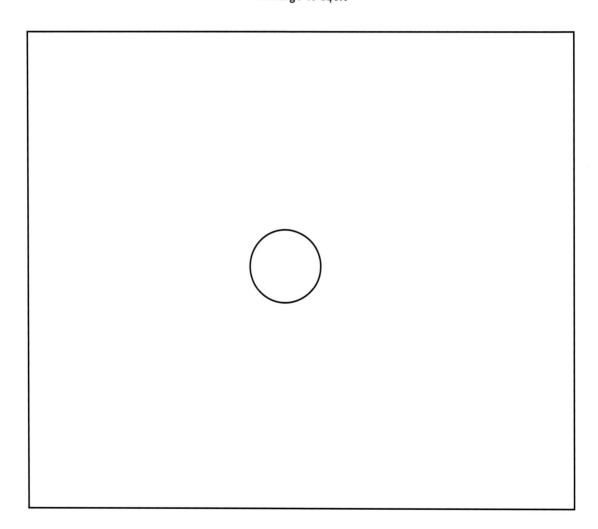

FRONT

Enlarge to 140%

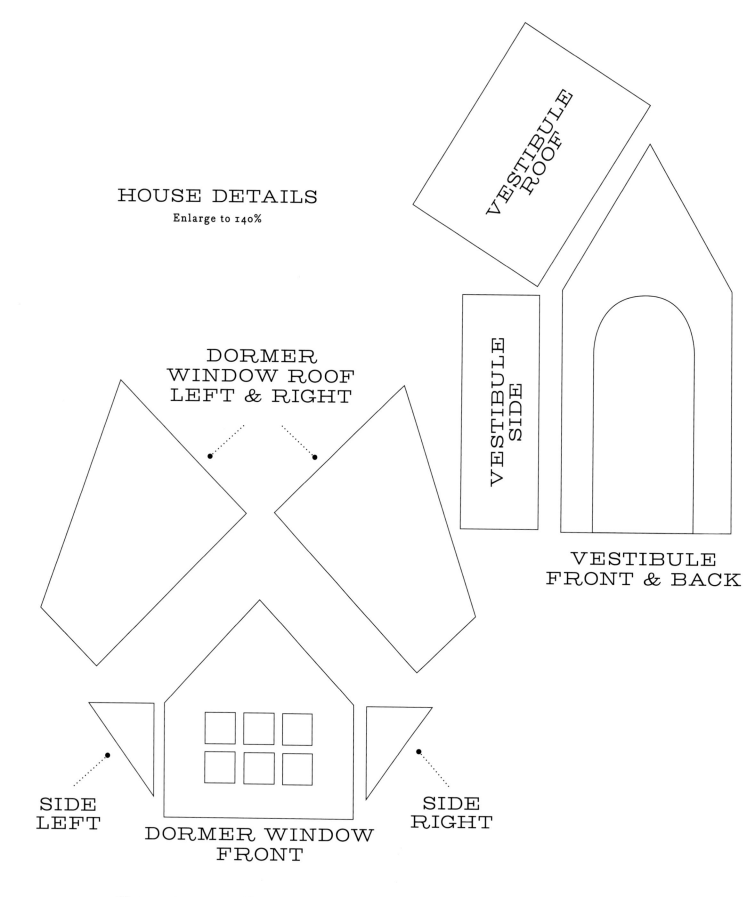

HOUSE DETAILS

Enlarge to 140%

VESTIBULE ROOF

VESTIBULE SIDE

VESTIBULE FRONT & BACK

DORMER WINDOW ROOF LEFT & RIGHT

SIDE LEFT

SIDE RIGHT

DORMER WINDOW FRONT

WINTER WONDERLAND

HOUSE DETAILS

Enlarge to 140%

FENCE

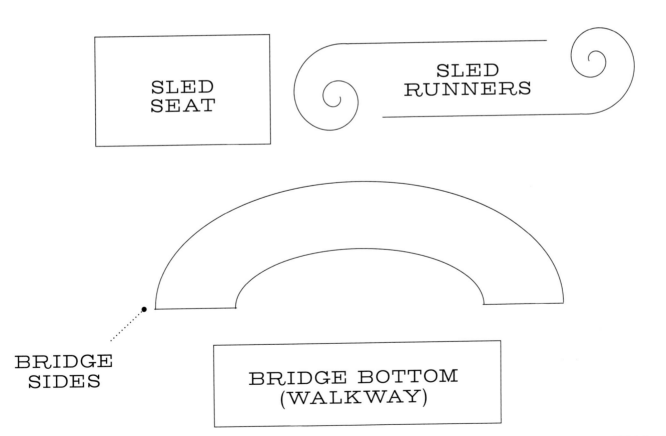

SLED SEAT

SLED RUNNERS

BRIDGE SIDES

BRIDGE BOTTOM (WALKWAY)

SIDE

Enlarge to 140%

ROOF

Enlarge to 140%

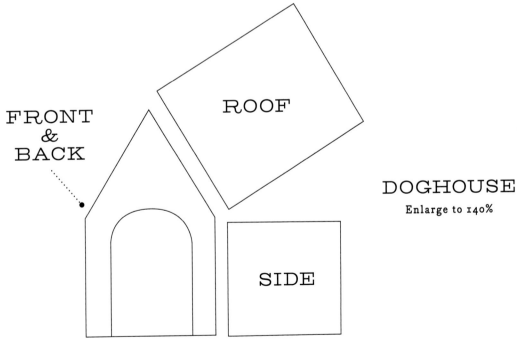

FRONT
&
BACK

ROOF

DOGHOUSE

Enlarge to 140%

SIDE

SWEET RETREAT

Enlarge to 140%

FRONT & BACK

ROOF
Enlarge to 140%

SIDE
Enlarge to 140%

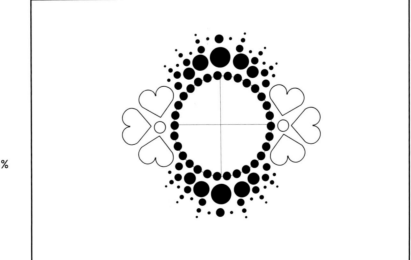

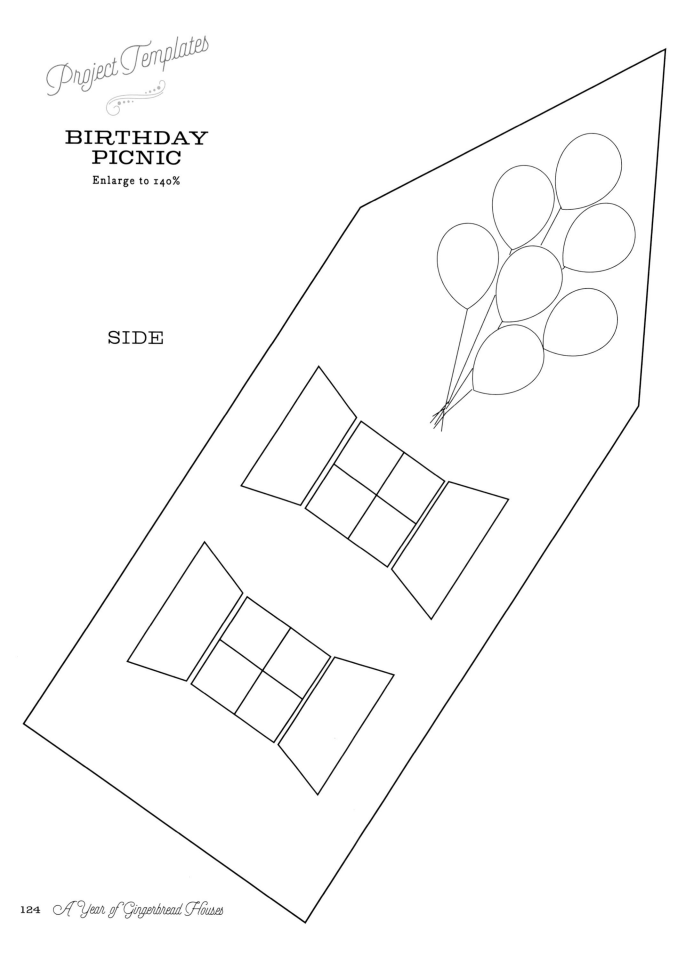

BIRTHDAY PICNIC

Enlarge to 140%

SIDE

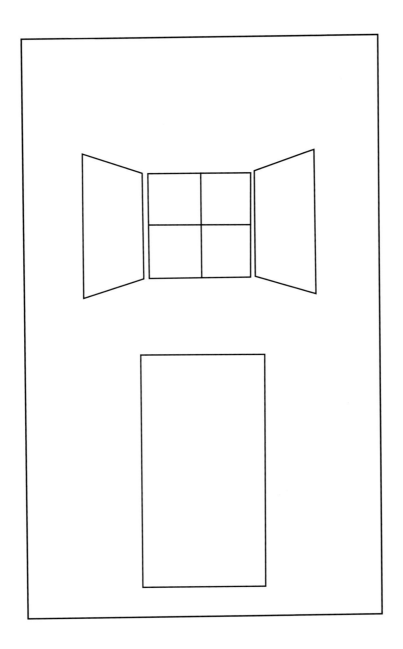

FRONT & BACK
Enlarge to 140%

HOUSE DETAILS

Enlarge to 140%

DOOR
STEPS

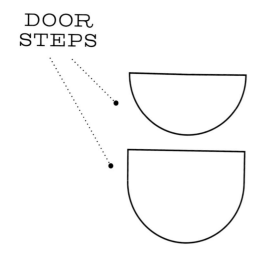

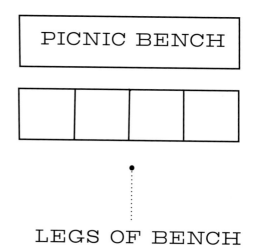

LEGS OF BENCH

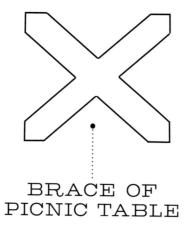

BRACE OF
PICNIC TABLE

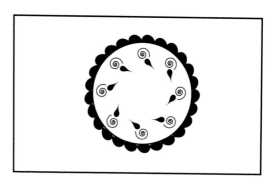

TOP OF
PICNIC TABLE

ROOF

Enlarge to 140%

Enlarge to 130%

Enlarge to 130%

Resources

ONLINE SUPPLIERS

Country Kitchen Sweet Art
www.countrykitchensa.com
Coarse sugar, sprinkles, impression mats, plunger cutters, silicone molds, cookie cutters, etc.

Global Sugar Art
www.globalsugarart.com

Sugarcraft
www.sugarcraft.com
Frill and garret cutters (FMM Straight Frill Cutter Set 9–12), small impression mats (cobblestone and woodgrain)

Wilton Cake Decorating
www.wilton.com

Cake Supplies 4 U
www.cakesupplies4u.com

Sugar Gypsy by Ruth Rickey
www.sugar-gypsy.myshopify.com

Mold Muse
www.moldmuse.com
Silicone molds

Clay Alley (Kemper Cutters)
www.clayalley.com

BOOKS & WEBSITES

Gingerbread Houses: Baking and Building Memories, by Nonnie Cargas

Gingerbread Academy: Techniques of Hungarian Gingerbread, by Tunde Dugantsi and Aniko Vargane Orban

Gingerbread for All Seasons, by Teresa Layman

Gingerbread: Things to Make and Bake, by Teresa Layman and Barbara Morgenroth

Making Great Gingerbread Houses: Delicious Designs from Cabins to Castles, from Lighthouses to Tree Houses, by Aaron Morgan and Paige Gilchrist

Sweet Dreams of Gingerbread, by Jann Johnson

The Gingerbread Book, by Steven Stellingwerf

The Gingerbread Book: 54 Cookie-Construction Projects for Party Centerpieces and Holiday Decorations, 117 Full-Sized Patterns, Plans for 18 Structures, over 100 Color Photos, Recipes, Cookie Shapes, Children's Projects, History, and Step-by-Step How-To's, edited by Allen Bragdon

The Gingerbread Architect: Recipes and Blueprints for Twelve Classic American Homes, by Susan Matheson and Lauren Chattman

Julia M. Usher's Ultimate Cookies, by Julia M. Usher

The Gingerbread Journal
www.gingerbreadjournal.com

Julie Usher's Cookie Connection
www.cookieconnection.juliausher.com

Tunde's Creations
www.tundescreations.com

LilaLoa—by Georganne
www.lilaloa.com

The Sweet Adventures of Sugar Belle
www.sweetsugarbelle.com

Sweetopia Decorating Cookies, Cupcakes, Cakes and . . .
www.sweetopia.net

Haniela's
www.hanielas.com

My Little Bakery
www.cakecreationsforyou.blogspot.com

Index

Acknowledgments

To Mom, who inspired and encouraged my love of baking and gingerbread at a very young age. I will forever remember the hours we spent in the kitchen together, and your encouragement, love, and gentle advice continue to shape me. Your creative, charming, flawless creations graced our home, and our hearts, every year.

To Dad, who has unwrapped a mountain of sweet tarts and let us stay up late while Mom baked!

To my husband Jonathan—for your patience, love, friendship, and encouragement. I couldn't have done this without your help managing our family while I baked, iced, wrote, and photographed. Thanks for all the nights we ate take-out on one corner of a gingerbread-encrusted table. You are my number one fan, critic, and gumdrop thief. You're my love, and our children's hero.

To Nathan and Natalie, for being your own glorious selves and not cookie-cutter kids (ha ha). While I worked you sang, played piano, memorized scripts, read to me, listened to Danny the Champion of the World five times, and told me way too many knock-knock jokes. You stood by, always on alert, ready and willing to consume misshapen candies. Thanks for making the cookie dirt. I love and adore you both to infinity and beyond, plus two.

To Ruth Rickey, for her technical editing skills and for sharing her talent and enthusiasm with so many. Ruth is one of those people you sincerely wish lived in the house next door. My short class time with you was valuable beyond words.

To Shannon O'Hara, for transforming our home into a photo studio and for stunning photos that show the world in its best light. Anyone looking for a photographer with artistic vision, patience, diplomacy, professional excellence, and an indefatigable work ethic should give this man a call. You're welcome back anytime.

To Jennifer Williams, Kimberly Broderick, Yeon Kim, Chris Thompson, Jen Cogliantry, Chris Bain, and the rest of the team at Sterling Publishing. You have guided me through this adventure with patience, encouragement, and expert advice. Every novice author should be so lucky.

To Bridget Edwards, for sharing her own journey as an author with me, and for her masterful, enthusiastic blogging. Her blog demonstrates a generosity of spirit and a willingness to teach sugarcraft to anyone with the bandwidth and a spatula. Know that she was equally generous in answering my questions.

To Lori Paximadis, for detailed copyediting and asking the right questions to clarify the text. The book is better for it.

About the Author

Kristine Samuell started her baking adventures at her mother's elbow, peering in wonder at her gingerbread masterpieces. Many bags of flour later, Kristine still loves to create houses for holidays, special occasions, and charity auctions. Visit her blog, www.GingerbreadJournal.com, for updates and ideas. Kristine lives in Texas with her husband and two children, all of whom wished to title the book, "Don't eat that! It's for the gingerbread house."